THE LEARNING AND TEACHING OF ALGEBRA

The Learning and Teaching of Algebra provides a pedagogical framework for the teaching and learning of algebra grounded in theory and research.

Areas covered include:

- Algebra: Setting the Scene
- Some Lessons From History
- Seeing Algebra Through the Eyes of a Learner
- Emphases in Algebra Teaching
- Algebra Education in the Digital Era

This guide will be essential reading for trainee and qualified teachers of mathematics, graduate students, curriculum developers, researchers and all those who are interested in the "problématique" of teaching and learning algebra. It allows you to get involved in the wealth of knowledge that teachers can draw upon to assist learners, helping you gain the insights that mastering algebra provides.

Abraham Arcavi holds the Lester B. Pearson Professorial Chair at the Weizmann Institute of Science, Israel. He has written about the teaching and learning of algebra for researchers and teachers, led large curriculum development projects, and has been involved in teacher professional development for more than 30 years.

Paul Drijvers is Professor of Mathematics Education at the Freudenthal Institute, Utrecht University, The Netherlands. His research interests include the role of ICT in mathematics education, the teaching and learning of algebra, and teachers' professional development.

Kaye Stacey is Professor Emeritus at the University of Melbourne, Australia, having held the Foundation Chair of Mathematics Education there for 20 years. She has made major contributions to understanding students' early learning of formal algebra and discovering how information technology can enhance the teaching of algebra and functions throughout secondary school.

IMPACT (Interweaving Mathematics Pedagogy and Content for Teaching)

IMPACT (Interweaving Mathematics Pedagogy and Content for Teaching) is an exciting new series of texts for teacher education which aims to advance the learning and teaching of mathematics by integrating mathematics content with the broader research and theoretical base of mathematics education.

The Learning and Teaching of Algebra
Ideas, Insights, and Activities
Abraham Arcavi, Paul Drijvers, and Kaye Stacey

THE LEARNING AND TEACHING OF ALGEBRA

Ideas, Insights, and Activities

*Abraham Arcavi, Paul Drijvers,
and Kaye Stacey*

LONDON AND NEW YORK

First published 2017
by Routledge
2 Park Square, Milton Park, Abingdon, Oxon OX14 4RN

and by Routledge
711 Third Avenue, New York, NY 10017

Routledge is an imprint of the Taylor & Francis Group, an informa business

© 2017 Abraham Arcavi, Paul Drijvers, and Kaye Stacey

The right of Abraham Arcavi, Paul Drijvers, and Kaye Stacey to be identified as authors of this work has been asserted by them in accordance with sections 77 and 78 of the Copyright, Designs and Patents Act 1988.

All rights reserved. No part of this book may be reprinted or reproduced or utilized in any form or by any electronic, mechanical, or other means, now known or hereafter invented, including photocopying and recording, or in any information storage or retrieval system, without permission in writing from the publishers.

Trademark notice: Product or corporate names may be trademarks or registered trademarks, and are used only for identification and explanation without intent to infringe.

British Library Cataloguing in Publication Data
A catalogue record for this book is available from the British Library

Library of Congress Cataloging in Publication Data
Names: Arcavi, Abraham. | Drijvers, Paul (Paulus Hendrikus Maria), 1958- | Stacey, Kaye, 1948-
Title: The learning and teaching of algebra : ideas, insights. and activities / Abraham Arcavi, Paul Drijvers, and Kaye Stacey.
Description: Abingdon, Oxon ; New York, NY : Routledge, 2017. | Includes bibliographical references.
Identifiers: LCCN 2016005953| ISBN 9780415743693 (hardback) | ISBN 9780415743723 (pbk.) | ISBN 9781315545189 (ebook)
Subjects: LCSH: Algebra--Study and teaching.
Classification: LCC QA152.3 .A27 2017 | DDC 512.9071--dc23
LC record available at https://lccn.loc.gov/2016005953

ISBN: 978-0-415-74369-3 (hbk)
ISBN: 978-0-415-74372-3 (pbk)
ISBN: 978-1-315-54518-9 (ebk)

Typeset in Bembo and Stone Sans
by Saxon Graphics Ltd, Derby

To students, teachers, and teacher educators, hoping that this book will contribute to making the learning of algebra productive, enjoyable, and accessible to all.

CONTENTS

Acknowledgments   ix
IMPACT – Series Foreword   xi
Preface   xiii

1   Algebra—Setting the Scene   1
    1.1 *Introduction* 1
    1.2 *Algebra—Aims, Actions, and Entities* 1
    1.3 *Why Algebra?* 16
    1.4 *Chapter Summary* 19
    1.5 *Thinking Further* 20
    1.6 *References* 22

2   Some Lessons From History   25
    2.1 *Introduction* 25
    2.2 *Linear Equations in Ancient Egypt* 26
    2.3 *Quadratic Equations in Ancient Babylonia* 31
    2.4 *A Geometric View of Algebra From Arabic Mathematics* 33
    2.5 *Beyond Solving Equations: The Emergence of Algebra in Europe* 37
    2.6 *Chapter Summary* 41
    2.7 *Thinking Further* 42
    2.8 *References* 47

3   Seeing Algebra Through the Eyes of a Learner   48
    3.1 *Introduction—Putting on Teachers' Bifocal Spectacles* 48
    3.2 *What Do Algebraic Letters Represent?* 50
    3.3 *The Process–Object Duality* 53

3.4 The Meaning of the Equals Sign 55
3.5 Algebra for Recording and Revealing Mathematical Structure 56
3.6 Transitions From Learning Arithmetic to Learning Algebra 58
3.7 The Procedures of Equation Solving 64
3.8 Functions as Processes and Objects 69
3.9 Chapter Summary 72
3.10 Thinking Further 73
3.11 References 77

4 Emphases in Algebra Teaching 80
4.1 Introduction 80
4.2 Teaching Algebra in Context 81
4.3 Productive Practice 87
4.4 The Reconciliation of Routine and Insight 90
4.5 Exploiting Student Mistakes 95
4.6 Proofs in Algebra Teaching 99
4.7 Chapter Summary 101
4.8 Thinking Further 102
4.9 References 104

5 Algebra Education in the Digital Era 106
5.1 Introduction 106
5.2 Digital Tools for Algebra 108
5.3 Core Algebra Entities With Digital Means 118
5.4 Teaching and Learning Algebra With Digital Means 127
5.5 Chapter Summary 130
5.6 Thinking Further 132
5.7 References 134

Epilogue 136
Index 140

ACKNOWLEDGMENTS

We acknowledge with gratitude the support of the Weizmann Institute of Science, the Freudenthal Institute at Utrecht University, and the University of Melbourne. We thank Nathalie Kuijpers for her careful and thorough assistance with editing of the manuscript. We were fortunate that the IMPACT series editors, Tommy Dreyfus, Frank K. Lester, and Günter Törner, invited us to work together on this project, thereby establishing for us an enjoyable and instructive international collaboration and exchange of ideas. The final manuscript benefitted from the insightful comments of two reviewers.

IMPACT – SERIES FOREWORD

IMPACT, an acronym for *Interweaving Mathematics Pedagogy And Content for Teaching*, is a series of textbooks dedicated to mathematics education and suitable for teacher education. The leading principle of the series is the integration of mathematics content with topics from research on mathematics learning and teaching. Elements from the history and the philosophy of mathematics, as well as curricular issues are integrated as appropriate.

Whereas in mathematics there are many textbook series representing internationally accepted canonical curricula, such a series has so far been lacking in mathematics education. It is the intention of IMPACT, to fill this gap.

The books in the series will focus on fundamental conceptual understanding of the central ideas and relationships, while often compromising on the breadth of coverage. These central ideas and relationships will serve as organizers for the structure of each book. Beyond being an integrated presentation of the central ideas of mathematics and their learning and teaching, the volumes will serve as guides to further resources.

The first volume in the series treats Algebra, a central topic in any high school mathematics curriculum around the world, and a topic with inherent complexities due to factors such as the increasing numbers of students who are expected to learn algebra, and to opportunities for new ways of doing algebra provided by technological change. Hence a coherent view of the central ideas and relationships that integrates algebra content with the main issues and results from research appeared particularly crucial, leading to the choice of Algebra as topic of the first volume in the series.

Series editors
Tommy Dreyfus (Israel), Frank K. Lester (USA),
Günter Törner (Germany)

Series Advisory Board

Abraham Arcavi (Israel), Michèle Artigue (France), Jo Boaler (USA), Hugh Burkhardt (Great Britain), Willi Dörfler (Austria), Koeno Gravemeijer (The Netherlands), Angel Gutierrez (Spain), Gabriele Kaiser (Germany), Carolyn Kieran (Canada), Jeremy Kilpatrick (USA), Jürg Kramer (Germany), Fou-Lai Lin (Republic of China - Taiwan), John Monaghan (Great Britain/Norway), Mogens Niss (Denmark), Alan H. Schoenfeld (USA), Peter Sullivan (Australia), Michael O. J. Thomas (New Zealand) and Patrick W. Thompson (USA)

PREFACE

This book addresses the problématique of the teaching and learning of school algebra.

"Problématique" is a word borrowed from the French and it describes not just problems in isolation, but comprehensive challenges posed by a certain large-scale theme. In other words, it consists of articulating questions and dilemmas arising in a certain area. The problématique addressed by this book can be posed in general terms as follows. On the one hand, algebra is considered a central subject to be studied in junior high and high schools in almost all educational systems around the world. The reasons for this centrality may vary considerably (see Section 1.3) but the consensus is that time and effort should be devoted to its teaching and learning. On the other hand, students have serious cognitive and affective difficulties with algebra, that is, they have difficulties in becoming competent at it and even if they succeed, many fail to see the point of studying it.

This book addresses the problématique of teaching and learning school algebra on the basis of knowledge accumulated by decades of research and development work by mathematicians, mathematics educators and mathematics education researchers during the last five decades. That work will be succinctly evoked as a springboard to propose additional ideas and suggestions illustrated by thought-provoking annotated examples.

This book is intended as a useful and lively resource for mathematics teachers, teacher educators, student teachers (including those in career shifting programs), curriculum developers, and graduate students, and it can also be of interest to parents and students.

Chapter 1 describes the problématique and the essence of algebra: its aims, actions, and entities and dwells upon the question of why all students should learn algebra.

Chapter 2 provides brief historical snapshots describing how the main ideas and entities of school algebra came into being, and how algebraic symbolism (which is relatively recent as compared to Euclidean geometry) facilitated the solution of problems and accelerated the development of all areas of mathematics. Some lessons for mathematics education are discussed.

Chapter 3 centers on the learning of algebra by bringing in the students' perspective, their readiness (or lack of it) to cope with the main ideas of algebra, their difficulties, and sense making of algebraic problems.

Chapter 4 addresses teaching dilemmas and concerns such as: how to teach algebra in context, how to practice, how to reconcile procedural fluency and algebraic insight, how to tackle well-known student difficulties, and how to deal with proofs in algebra.

Chapter 5 addresses the affordances, opportunities, and challenges posed by new technologies and their roles in the wise use of the unprecedented computational power, in re-prioritizing goals and in re-sequencing the curriculum. Different approaches to how these technologies can be harnessed are described.

The Epilogue presents conclusions and recommendations.

Throughout the book, annotated examples are presented to illustrate the main claims made. A section entitled "Thinking Further" is included at the end of each chapter. It includes suggestions for discussions and activities in pre-service or in-service teacher education workshops, forums, and teacher deliberations in departmental or professional meetings. This section also includes some mathematical tasks related to the contents of the chapter in order to enhance and extend the points made therein.

1
ALGEBRA—SETTING THE SCENE

> Saying what algebra "is" is not a minor problem.
> (Lins, 2011, p. 38)

> I don't know much about algebra, but who cares?
> (Student quoted by House, 1988, p. 3)

1.1 Introduction

This chapter dwells upon two main issues: the specific aims, actions, and entities of algebra and the question of why all students should learn algebra. As such it sets the scene for the following chapters in which aims, actions, and entities as well as the "why" question are further discussed and exemplified.

1.2 Algebra—Aims, Actions, and Entities

1.2.1 Aims

Talking about the aims of algebra is tantamount to attempting to provide an answer to the question "what is algebra, and what is it for?" Despite Lins' (2011) observation above that it is difficult to put into words what algebra is, and that "there is no Supreme Court to decide such questions" (Freudenthal, 1977, p. 193), we review some proposed answers.

The word algebra became widespread in the mid-16th century and it derives from the Arabic "Al Jabr" (or Al Jebr) as it was used by the mathematician Muhammad ibn Musa al-Khwarizmi in the title of his famous treatise on equations "Kitab al-Jabr w'al-Muqabala"—"Rules of Reintegration and Reduction" or

"Restoring and Balancing" (Online Etymology Dictionary, 2001–2015). Thus, the etymology of the word evokes the main rules for solving equations.

The word algebra nowadays indicates diverse areas within mathematics such as school ("elementary") algebra, linear algebra, and abstract algebra. The word "algebra" is also used to denote a specific structure (e.g. "an algebra over a field," "Lie Algebra"). Sometimes it stands for operations and methods of calculations involving symbols, as in commonly heard expressions such as "do the algebra!" (Wikipedia, Algebra, 2015). Throughout this book, we refer only to algebra taught at school and the following are some of the definitions that can be applied to it.

> the branch of mathematics that deals with general statements of relations, utilizing letters and other symbols to represent specific sets of numbers, values, vectors, etc., in the description of such relations.
> *(Dictionary.reference.com, 2012)*

> the branch of mathematics that deals with symbolizing general numerical relationships and mathematical structures and with operating on those structures.
> *(Kieran, 1992, p. 391)*

> the art of manipulating sums, products, and powers of [all] numbers … the manipulations may be carried out with letters standing for the numbers … the rules even apply to things … An algebraic system is … a set of elements of any sort on which … addition and multiplication operate, provided only that these operations satisfy certain rules.
> *(Mac Lane & Birkhoff, 1967, p. 1)*

> algebra involves … investigating number systems and their operations … operating with variables, solving equations, creating formulas for problem situations (algebrafication), working with functions in terms of formulas, tables and graphs, finding derivatives …
> *(Drijvers, Goddijn & Kindt, 2011, p. 7)*

> the basic ingredients of school algebra [are]: generalization of numerical and geometrical patterns and of the laws governing numerical relationships, problem solving, functional situations and modelling of physical and mathematical phenomena.
> *(Kieran, 2004, p. 21)*

This sample of definitions is far from being exhaustive and it suggests a range of aims of algebra, which we will subsequently discuss:

- Expressing generalizations
- Establishing relationships

- Solving problems
- Exploring properties
- Proving theorems
- Calculating.

Expressing generalizations, that is, using letters to represent numbers (or other mathematical objects) in order to handle at once whole classes of numbers (or of other objects) to express a pattern or a relationship. Consider the example described in Figure 1.1. Algebra is an ideal tool to express the generalization requested.

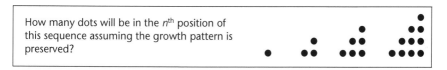

FIGURE 1.1 Example of generalization of a pattern of dot arrangements.

Establishing relationships (some of which are functions) between numbers or quantities by means of words, formulas, tables, or graphs. For example, the relation between the amount to be paid after filling the petrol tank of a car and the amount of petrol filled can be expressed by $y = ax$, where y is the amount to be paid, x is the amount of petrol, and a is the price per unit (litre or gallon). If there is an extra fixed fee to be paid independently of the amount filled (for example, a night fee), say b, the relationship becomes $y = ax + b$.

Solving problems involving unknowns linked by operations in equations or inequalities. These problems can be posed as pure mathematical situations or in the context of modeling real life situations (in order to find answers to questions inherent to the situation). Consider, for example the problem posed in Figure 1.2.

> The petrol station MM charges 3 dollars per gallon regardless of the time of the day, the petrol station PP charges 2.9 dollars but adds an extra 1 dollar fee if you buy it between 9pm and 6am. In which service station will you save money if you buy petrol at 11 pm?

FIGURE 1.2 Example of a problem to be solved with algebra.

Solving the equation $3x = 2.9x + 1$ gives the number of gallons at which PP starts to become cheaper.

Exploring properties of operations defined by formal rules. For an example see Figure 1.3.

> We define the operation $\oplus$ as producing the arithmetic mean of any two numbers, namely $a \oplus b = \frac{a+b}{2}$. Does the associative law hold for this operation? Or in other words, is the equality $(a \oplus b) \oplus c = a \oplus (b \oplus c)$ true for all numbers?

FIGURE 1.3 Exploring a property of an operation.

Proving theorems at school is mostly confined to geometry. However, algebra can provide many opportunities to apply deductive reasoning and at the same time establish general theorems. Consider the conjecture in Figure 1.4. This was proposed by a student in a mathematics class (Sherzer, 1973) without knowing that it had already been presented by the French mathematician Chuquet (1445–1488); nowadays it is known as the *Mediant Inequality*.

> Given two fractions $\frac{a}{b} < \frac{c}{d}$ ($a,b,c,d > 0$), prove that $\frac{a}{b} < \frac{a+c}{b+d} < \frac{c}{d}$

FIGURE 1.4 The Mediant Inequality.

Elementary number theory also provides many theorems to prove with algebra. Consider, for example, the proof that the sum of five consecutive numbers is always a multiple of 5.

Calculating. Whereas a main aim of arithmetic (if not its only one) is calculating, school algebra aspires to much more, as illustrated by the aims above. However, by virtue of its power to symbolically display general relations and structure, it also contributes to better understanding of calculation methods and even to creating new efficient and elegant methods. Consider ways to calculate 98^2, using the property $(a - b)^2 = a^2 - 2ab + b^2$, i.e. $(100 - 2)^2 = 100^2 - 2 \times 100 \times 2 + 2^2$, or the property $a^2 - b^2 = (a + b)(a - b)$, i.e. $98^2 - 2^2 = (98 + 2)(98 - 2)$. The calculation becomes very easy and can be done mentally. Also, consider the following claim: "The square of a two digit number ending in 5 always ends in 25 preceded by the product of its tens digits with its successor." For example, 65^2 ends in 25 preceded by $6 \times 7 = 42$, namely 4225. This method can be easily justified using algebra.

1.2.2 Actions

What is it that we actually do with algebra? What are the physical and mental actions we engage in when we "do algebra"? In the following we describe the main actions involved:

- Noticing, describing, denoting, and representing
- Handling symbolic expressions
- "Unsymbolizing" and reading

Algebra—Setting the Scene 5

- Connecting representations
- Creating algebraic expressions.

Noticing, describing, denoting, and representing regularities and patterns can be done by means of words, symbols, tables, or graphs. Consider the problem posed in Figure 1.5.

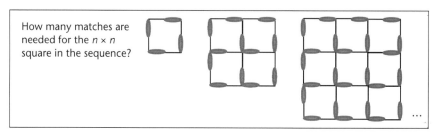

FIGURE 1.5 Example of noticing, describing, denoting, and representing patterns.

Observation would result in noticing what stays the same throughout the sequence and what changes and how. For example, it may be noticed (a) that the shapes are always squares, (b) there is a regular (linear) increase in the number of matches, and (c) the need to resist an initial tendency to calculate the total number of matches by multiplying the number of small (unit) squares by four (since internal matches would be counted twice). Some people may attempt to find the general case by counting some special cases, as indicated in Figure 1.6, and trying to generalize.

Square size	Number of matches
1 × 1	4
2 × 2	12
3 × 3	24
4 × 4	40
5 × 5	60

FIGURE 1.6 Number of matches for some special cases.

Many others will proceed to notice, describe, and represent the patterns on the basis of visually perceived regularities. For example, noticing the mistake of counting matches twice which we may avoid by decomposing the configuration as shown in Figure 1.7.

6 Algebra—Setting the Scene

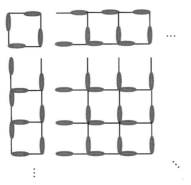

FIGURE 1.7 A decomposition of the general square.

This decomposition helps noticing that there is one shape that uses four matches, two chains (in the sides) containing $n - 1$ shapes using three matches and $(n - 1)(n - 1)$ shapes using two matches, and thus the total number needed for a $n \times n$ square is $2(n^2 + n)$.

Hershkowitz, Arcavi, and Bruckheimer (2001) illustrate several strategies based on noticing, describing, and representing patterns that support solving this task. It is worth noticing that different ways of counting may yield different forms of the algebraic expression, and thus we can engage in showing that these expressions are equivalent (in the sense described in Section 1.2.3) by handling them using algebraic properties in order to transform one into the other. For a similar example see Section 4.2.

Handling symbolic expressions according to algebraic rules, with a certain purpose (e.g. substituting numbers for variables, simplifying, solving), is a most common action in algebra especially in the context of solving equations. For example, consider solving the following equation (de Guzmán, 1995, p. 114):

$$x^2 + \left(\frac{x}{x+1}\right)^2 = 1$$

An initial start could be to expand the expression and look for an equivalent equation for which we may have a ready-made way to solve. However, after some procedural work, one notices that this is a fourth degree equation, which is quite complicated to solve in its expanded form. If the main objective is to quickly obtain the roots of the equation, one can certainly feed it into a computer algebra system. However, if the goal is not only to reach a solution, but also to find a way to solve it, the challenge is to handle this equation using algebraic rules and properties in order to find a simpler equivalent one. With this purpose in mind, we can play around with the rules. One may be tempted to view the left-hand side as an incomplete trinomial and attempt to complete the square to achieve an expression of the form $(a + b)^2$ by adding the same term to both sides. Trials may be unconducive, but this trialing may suggest considering also the form $(a - b)^2$ as a target, and this is productive:

$$x^2 + \left(\frac{x}{x+1}\right)^2 - 2\left(\frac{x^2}{x+1}\right) = 1 - 2\left(\frac{x^2}{x+1}\right) \Rightarrow \left(\frac{x^2}{x+1}\right)^2 = 1 - 2\left(\frac{x^2}{x+1}\right)$$

The substitution $t = \frac{x^2}{x+1}$ yields a quadratic equation in t whose solution poses a new quadratic equation in x. This example illustrates purposeful handling of algebraic procedures—simplification, completion of expressions, substitution of variables—without having a specific recipe to follow. The properties to apply have to be tried in order to establish their productiveness. This task may be difficult for beginners but it exemplifies pervasive actions that can be performed also with simpler examples.

Sometimes, rather than simplifying an expression, the purpose of handling a symbolic expression can be the opposite, that is to "complexify" it. For example, consider the "Broken Calculator" (Teachscape, n.d.). In such a calculator, the + key is disabled, and yet the task consists of calculating the sum of two large numbers, for example, 5678 + 9876, with this calculator anyway. This is another example in which we can resort to algebra for a purpose. The problem is tantamount to the question: can we express a sum by means of some combination of the other operations, available in a simple calculator? Algebra suggests the use of some properties to "complexify" the simple expression of addition in order to find several possibilities, such as: $2a - (a - b)$ or $\frac{a^2 - b^2}{a - b}$.

Unsymbolizing and reading consists of the inspection of algebraic expressions in order to extract information from them, as exemplified in Figure 1.8.

When three students were requested to find how many cells there are in the shaded border of an $n \times n$ grid, they produced the following expressions:

$2n + 2(n - 2)$, $4(n - 1)$ and $4(n - 2) + 4$.

Describe how the counting was performed in each case in order to yield such equations.

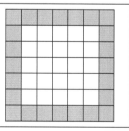

FIGURE 1.8 Reconstructing the creation of given expressions.

This task requires inspecting the expressions in order to reconstruct the counting processes they reflect. We can proceed, for example, by parsing the expressions as follows. In the case of $4(n - 1)$ there must be four sets, each of them having $(n - 1)$ unit squares: each of these sets is made of one corner and the non-corner unit squares of a side. Similarly, in the case of $2n + 2(n - 2)$, we should be looking for two sets with n unit squares (e.g. the top and bottom) and another two sets with $(n - 2)$ (e.g. the vertical sides without the corners).

8 Algebra—Setting the Scene

Sometimes the action of carefully "reading into" an algebraic equation or expression is not tied to the process of its construction, but may be useful to reduce the number of algebraic procedures needed. Consider solving the following equation:

$$\frac{x^2-1}{x^2+1} = x^2+1$$

Reading the expressions that form this equation may include following Freudenthal's (1983, p. 469) advice to reject the truism "when calculating starts, thinking finishes" and to unblock our ways back to insight. In this case, it would consist of noticing that the left-hand side of the equation always represents a number smaller than 1 (since the numerator of the fractional expression is always smaller than its denominator), whereas the right-hand side is always a number greater than 1. Therefore, this equation cannot have real solutions. The action of reading an expression not only saves procedural work (which is often prone to error), but it also reconnects us with the relations depicted in the algebraic equation. This may be an antidote to the widespread perception that algebra comes down to meaningless application of ritualistic procedures.

Connecting representations consists of using multiple representations in order to deploy ideas and concepts, to operate upon them, to discern nuances, and to engender new knowledge about mathematical content (e.g. diSessa, Hammer, & Sherin, 1991). Translating within and between representations may also influence both grasping a concept and generating a solution to a problem. Consider slope, a main concept intrinsic to linear functions as expressing its constant rate of change. Symbolically, slope is "the number that multiplies the x in $f(x) = ax + b$" and graphically it is "the measurement of the steepness of the line in a Cartesian coordinate plane" as well as the ratio "rise over run." In a table in which the differences in the independent variable are equal to 1, the slope is the difference in consecutive values of the dependent variable. A central action in algebra may consist of explicating the connection between the number multiplying the variable in the symbolic expression for a linear function and the measurement of the steepness of the line that represents it in the Cartesian coordinate plane.

Consider the problem posed in Figure 1.9.

What do all linear functions of the form $f(x) = ax + a$ have in common?

FIGURE 1.9 A problem related to slope.

The symbolic solution would imply a simple syntactic transformation and its interpretation: $f(x) = ax + a = a(x + 1)$ and thus regardless of the value of a, for all these functions, $f(-1) = 0$, namely they share the pair $(-1, 0)$. In contrast, consider the following graphical solution. In $f(x) = ax + a$, the first a is the slope, the second is the y-intercept. Since, graphically slope is "rise over run," and since in this case the value of the slope is the same as the value of the y-intercept, to a rise with the value of the y-intercept must correspond a run of 1 (this reasoning applies to both positive and negative values of *a*). Drawing such a "run" shows that the intersection point for all the functions in this family is (− 1,0). Whereas the algebraic solution does not engage the meanings of the parameters and it is concise and formal, the graphical solution resorts to the meanings of the parameters to deduce the same solution.

One can also introduce yet another visual representation in which the axes are parallel instead of orthogonal, and the independent variable is connected to the dependent variable by mapping segments. Thus, the role of the point in the Cartesian representation is now played by a segment (which can be extended to become a line). This representation is called the Parallel Axes Representation (PAR) and the comparison with the Cartesian representation yields interesting insights (see, for example, Arcavi & Nachmias, 1989). In Figure 1.10, the PAR representation of the function *f* with $f(x) = 2x + 1$ is shown.

How is slope depicted in this representation? This and many other issues can be explored by connecting this special PAR with the others. For example, in the bundle of mapping segments, what does the only horizontal segment represent (and, does it always exist and is it indeed the only one)? How is this represented in the graphical Cartesian and the symbolic representations? How is the y-intercept represented (note that this terminology is highly tied to the Cartesian coordinate plane, and has no special meaning in the PAR since all the mapping lines intercept the y-axis)? Also, it can be proven that, if extended as lines, all mapping segments intersect in one point. What is the relationship between the slope of the linear function and the position of that intersection point relative to the x-axis?

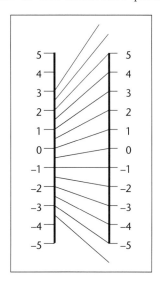

FIGURE 1.10 The Parallel Axes Representation of $f(x) = 2x + 1$.

10 Algebra—Setting the Scene

For more details see, for example, Arcavi & Nachmias (1993). Working with both the Cartesian representations and PARs demonstrates that connecting representations enhances the ways in which concepts are perceived, represented and understood.

Making connections between representations can also be a way of finding a solution to a problem which otherwise may be elusive or tortuous. Consider the problem posed in Figure 1.11.

Show that whenever $a + b + c = 1$ and $a - b + c = -2$, the quadratic equation $ax^2 + bc + c = 0$ has two different real roots.

FIGURE 1.11 A problem that becomes easily solvable when changing representations.

An elegant way to solve this problem consists of connecting two different mathematical entities (equations and functions), and their symbolic and graphical representations. If, instead of the equation, we consider the quadratic function $f(x) = ax^2 + bx + c$, the conditions $a + b + c = 1$ and $a - b + c = -2$ can be re-represented as $f(1) = 1$ and $f(-1) = -2$, respectively. Thus, the graph of the quadratic function, a parabola which hits a point in the first quadrant (1,1) and one in the third quadrant (−1,−2), must cross the x-axis twice. Therefore, the equation has two different real roots.

Creating expressions for a desired purpose is common in the initial stages of modeling: one has to decide on a variable to be chosen (e.g. Arcavi, 1994) and then create appropriate expressions, equations or inequalities to establish relationships that will be instrumental in solving the problem modeled. Consider the geometrical problem borrowed from Farrell and Ranucci (1973) shown in Figure 1.12.

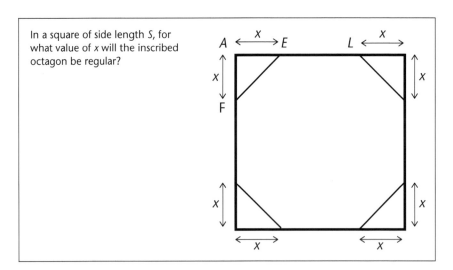

FIGURE 1.12 Creating expressions for modeling a problem.

In this problem, we can write the equation in two ways and one of them yields an extra root: a) by equating the lengths $EF = EL$ to obtain the linear equation in x, $S - 2x = \sqrt{2}\,x$, or b) in the triangle AEF, creating the following quadratic equation in x $(S - 2x)^2 = 2x^2$. Both equations solve the problem. However, the second yields an extra root, which may lead to interesting geometrical interpretations, absent from the first way of solving. Thus the creation of an equation in modeling a problem can be guided by expressing different relationships between the elements at stake and this can have implications in the interpretation of the solutions.

Creating expressions is not only required in the central context of modeling. It is possible to guide students to create expressions in very simple procedural exercises as well. Consider, for example, the exercise borrowed from Friedlander and Arcavi (2012) as shown in Figure 1.13. The creation process required is constrained to some conditions but at the same time it allows for freedom and for divergent thinking.

Complete the blanks (such that the equality holds):

___ + 6x + ___ = (___ + ___)²

___ + 6x + ___ = (___ + ___)²

___ + 6x + ___ = (___ + ___)²

FIGURE 1.13 Exercising the creation of equivalent expressions in different ways.

1.2.3 Entities

The objects by means of which algebraic actions are performed to pursue the aims are:

- Signs
- Variables
- Algebraic expressions
- Equations
- Relations and functions.

Signs most commonly used in algebra are $=, >, <, \geq, \leq, ()$ and sometimes also $\neq$ and $\cong$. Later on, students may also encounter other signs, such as $|\ldots|$ to indicate absolute value or the modulus of a number, expression or vector. Familiarity with some of these signs is gained already in early arithmetic. However, their use in algebra includes subtleties and nuances that are not always very explicit and are not as common in arithmetic (e.g. Freudenthal, 1983). This is discussed in depth in Section 3.4. In arithmetic, the equals sign is usually considered as an invitation to perform an operation whose result is required; in algebra, it may also have other meanings. Consider, for example, $(a - b)(a + b) = a^2 - b^2$, which yields

$a^2 - b^2 = (a - b)(a + b)$ when reversed. Both express the same equivalence, yet the directionality may provide a different feel—the former may be regarded as performing a symbolic operation based on the distributive law, whereas the latter may be seen as a factorization. Learning and teaching algebra implies re-adjusting, enhancing, and enlarging the connotations of such a sign in order to handle a multiplicity of senses which may vary according to the context.

Variable is a central concept in algebra with different meanings and different roles (e.g. Freudenthal, 1983; Usiskin, 1988). Even in countries that do not use the Latin alphabet in their ordinary language, variables are signified in algebra by Latin letters. Throughout this book we use a letter as a sign for a variable and use the word "symbol" more generally, for example to include operations (e.g. +, −). The use of letters implies a radical departure from the use of numerals, which are so familiar to students before they start learning algebra, and thus it poses several potential difficulties. Such difficulties and possible ways to cope with them are addressed in detail in Chapters 3 and 4, respectively.

Numerals represent a single number whereas letters can represent

> simultaneously, yet individually, many different numbers ... It is this property of simultaneous representations that we refer to when we call these literal symbols *variables*, knowing full well that some of these symbols may, depending on the context, represent single unknown numbers, or even constants! It is this property ... that gives mathematical language its capacity to make very general statements ... in a concise and unambiguous form.
> *(Wagner, 1983, p. 475)*

Variables stand for numbers, for example numbers of objects or quantities, but they can refer to numbers in different ways. As such, the concept of variable has multiple facets, which are not always distinguished by mathematicians but should be attended to quite closely in mathematics education. In line with a large body of literature (Bednarz, Kieran, & Lee, 1996; Küchemann, 1981; MacGregor & Stacey, 1993; Malle, 1993; Usiskin, 1988) we distinguish five facets of the concept of variable: a placeholder for a number, an unknown number, a varying quantity, a generalized number, and a parameter.

The first and probably most straightforward facet of variable is the *placeholder* for a numerical value. In this view, the variable is considered as an empty box, a container for numerical values, like an empty place in a calculator memory that can be filled by a specific value.

The second facet of variable is the *unknown* number. In this view, a letter is used to denote a yet unknown number that needs to be found, as is the usual situation when solving equations.

The third facet concerns the *varying quantity*. In this view, the literal symbol does not stand for one single unknown value, but for a process running through a domain of possible values. It involves some sense of motion or dynamics, and is usually related to input–output relationships or functions, in which we want to investigate the co-variation of dependent and independent variables. For example, the area A of a triangle can be expressed in terms of its base b and its height h, as $A = \frac{1}{2} b \times h$.

When the variable acts as a *generalized number*, it is used to describe general properties. The variable does not refer to one or more specific numerical values, whether known or unknown, but generalizes over the domain set. Consider, for example, the following mathematical statement: $a + b = b + a$. The letters a and b can take any value from a specified set of numbers and thus they are the means to formulate statements (laws, properties) that hold for all the objects they name (usually real numbers in the algebra taught at school). This facet of variables was labeled "polyvalent names" by Freudenthal (1983, p. 474).

A *parameter* is a higher order variable in the sense that its value determines the situation as a whole. For example, in $y = ax + b$ we think of x and y as the varying quantities for fixed (but unknown) a and b. The values of a and b can vary but they are locally (temporarily) thought of as fixed. A change in the parameter value (e.g. the value of a) will not just change a point, but the complete function, graph, or expression at stake. At this higher level, a parameter can play each of the above variable roles, but at its own level. In a slightly different sense, the name parameter may also refer to an "intermediate" variable that links two other variables. Consider, for example, the two equations used to represent a circle of radius 1: $x = \cos(t)$ and $y = \sin(t)$.

These facets of the concept of variable are crucial in the learning and teaching processes as well as in the use of digital tools for algebra, as shown in Chapters 3, 4, and 5.

Algebraic expression is a combination of numbers, letters, and signs of operations that is well formed according to the rules of algebraic syntax. Expressions can be constant (e.g. 2), linear (e.g., $x + 3$), polynomial (e.g., $x^5 + 5.1x^2$), rational (e.g., $\frac{x}{x^3 - 1.8}$), or other (e.g. $\sqrt{a^2 + 9}$, e^x, $\log(x + 2)$). Expressions can include one or more variables (e.g., $x^2 + y$).

Algebraic expressions acquire specific numerical values when numbers are substituted for the variables and the operations in the expression are performed. Such substitutions are allowed whenever the operations are defined (or when the domain of substitution is explicitly defined). For example, we can substitute any real number in $\frac{1}{x^2 + 1}$, but we cannot substitute all real numbers in, for example, the following expressions: $\frac{1}{x^2}$, x^{-1}, $\sqrt{1 - x}$, $\log(3 + x)$.

Two algebraic expressions are equivalent whenever the domains of substitution are identical for both, and all numbers allowed for substitution in the first expression yield the same result in the second, and vice versa. Consider the following pairs of equivalent expressions: $3(x + 2)$ and $3x + 6$, $x^2 - 9$ and $(x - 3)(x + 3)$, $\sqrt{x^2}$ and $|x|$, $(x^2)^3$ and x^6, $|a - 8|$ and $|8 - a|$. In order to show that two expressions are equivalent, we must show that the domains of substitution are identical and that one can transform one expression into the other by means of legitimate algebraic operations. This approach to equivalent expressions may not be fully taken into account when it comes to simplifying expressions using a computer algebra system. These systems generally ignore restrictions on the domain, usually warning about this, but sometimes leaving to the user the task of sorting out the relevant domain according to the context of the problem being resolved.

Expressions can be seen as processes and as objects. These perspectives as well as the associated difficulties students may encounter are discussed in detail in Chapter 3.

Equation is a central construct of algebra and it pervades all branches of mathematics. Algebraic equations are characterized as <algebraic expression> = <algebraic expression>. However, there many approaches to characterize equations and the following illustrate how different sources define equations.

> A mathematical statement stating that two or more quantities are the same as one another, also called an equality, formula, or identity.
> *(Wolfram MathWorld, 1999–2015)*

> A formula of the form $A = B$, where A and B are expressions that may contain one or several variables called unknowns, and "=" denotes the equality binary relation. Although written in the form of proposition, an equation is not a statement that is either true or false, but a problem consisting of finding the values, called solutions, that, when substituted for the unknowns, yield equal values of the expressions A and B.
> *(Wikipedia, equation, 2015)*

> A statement, usually written in symbols, that states the equality of two quantities or algebraic expressions, e.g., $x + 3 = 5$. The quantity $x + 3$, to the left of the equals sign (=), is called the left-hand, or first, member of the equation, that to the right (5) the right-hand, or second, member. A numerical equation is one containing only numbers, e.g., $2 + 3 = 5$. A literal equation is one that, like the first example, contains some letters (representing unknowns or variables). An identical equation is a literal equation that is true for every value of the variable, e.g., the equation $(x + 1)^2 = x^2 + 2x + 1$. A conditional equation (usually referred to simply as an equation) is a literal equation that is not true for all values of the variable, e.g., only the value 2 for x makes true the equation $x + 3 = 5$. To solve an equation is to find the value or values of the variable that satisfy it.
> *(Free Dictionary, 2003–2015)*

> An analytical form of the problem of investigating which values of variables in functions give equal results. The arguments on which the functions depend are usually called the unknowns, and the values of the unknowns for which the values of the function are equal are called the solutions of the equation; for such values of the unknowns one also says that they satisfy the given equation. A solution of an equation of the form $f(x) = 0$ is also called a root of $f(x)$.
> *(Encyclopedia of Mathematics, 2014)*

The highlighted words that capture the essence of the concept in these definitions are: equality, mathematical statement, proposition, formula, and analytical form. Each of these terms stresses a different nuance of the concept. Some definitions (e.g. the second one) characterize equations as problems to be solved or as questions awaiting an answer. According to this view, equations are not, in themselves, true or false, but rather an invitation to search for the values to be substituted for the letters such that the equality holds. There is a distinction between identities for which any value in the domain of definition satisfies the equality (a way of forming an identity is placing an equals sign between two equivalent expressions), and conditional equations, for which the equality holds for one, several or no values. Thus in identities the variables play the roles of generalized numbers and in conditional equations the role of unknowns. In formulas, they have a sense of varying quantity.

Relations and functions are means to state, produce, reproduce, and handle dependencies and correspondences between variables. Functions are a special kind of relation for which it is required that for each value of the independent variable there is one and only one value of the dependent variable. In algebra taught at school, the variables nearly always stand for numbers, but one can find functions in geometry (usually termed mappings, or transformations). In higher mathematics one may find operators, morphisms, functors, which are functions but not of numbers. Functions can be described in words (e.g. the square of a number), in symbols, by means of tables of values and by graphs. In school, the functions studied are usually of one variable and are denoted either by $f(x) =$ (expression in x) or $y =$ (expression in x), sometimes by using only the letter f and sometimes, also specifying the domain and codomain as in $f: \mathbb{R} \to \mathbb{R}$, followed by an algebraic expression involving variables (and sometimes parameters), numbers and operations. Sometimes the way one writes an algebraic expression drives the perception of the mathematical entity we deal with. Consider, for example, $x + y = 10$ and $y = 10 - x$. The former is likely to be viewed as an equation in two unknowns, both having a similar status. Furthermore, one can reason that in order for their sum to be constant, as one increases, the other must decrease by the same amount. The latter is likely to be viewed as describing a function, where the status of the letters differs: x is the independent variable and y depends on x. Thus, even simple procedural operations on algebraic entities may lead us to switch the way in which we perceive, interpret and understand the entities in front of us.

Equations can also be described as a comparison between the values of two functions, namely as a way of finding the independent variable for which the two dependent variables are equal. Such an approach enables graphical solutions of the equations by searching for the intersection points of the graphs of two functions.

Chapters 3, 4, and 5 expand on the learning and teaching of the notion of function and its different representations in regular as well as technology-based environments.

1.3 Why Algebra?

"What's the point of learning algebra in the first place?" (Gibson, n.d.). This is a very frequent question asked by many students all over the world. In this section we address this question. Any answer seems to be seeking a "sense of purpose." Is that sense of purpose present in school instruction, or in textbooks? An evaluation study (Project 2061, 2013) investigated this question. In order to answer it, some popular algebra textbooks in the United States were analyzed. The report states that out of the twelve programs evaluated on "conveying unit purpose," three did poorly, four did fairly, three were satisfactory, two were good, and none was excellent. If textbooks seem to fail to convey the purpose of algebra, we speculate that most classroom practices may fail as well.

Here are some of the main points that we propose to convey to students either through explicit conversations or through classroom work on examples and problems. A first simple answer to the question "Why should I learn algebra?" is that

> algebra is the beginning of a journey that gives you the skills to solve … complex problems … Algebra is a stepping stone to learning about this wonderful universe that we live in. With it you have the tools to understand a great many things and you also have the skills needed to continue on and learn Trigonometry and Calculus which are essential for exploring other types of problems and phenomena around us.
>
> *(Gibson, n.d.)*

Thus, algebra education "helps to prepare students for their subsequent education" (Drijvers, Goddijn, & Kindt, 2011, p. 24).

Second, some educators raise the learning of algebra and becoming competent at it to the status of a civil rights issue:

> algebra, once solely in place as the gatekeeper for higher math and the priesthood who gained access to it, now is the gatekeeper for citizenship; and people who don't have it are like the people who couldn't read and write in the industrial age.
>
> *(Moses & Cobb, 2001, p. 14)*

Thus the argument is that it is the obligation of any educational system to offer optimal opportunities to gain knowledge of algebra.

These answers may reassure educators about the centrality of algebra in the curriculum, but they may be insufficient to convince students as they imply postponing for the future the answer to a pressing question from the present. As elaborated in Chapter 3, students are in "a stage in the curriculum when the introduction of algebra may make simple things hard" (Tall and Thomas, 1991, p. 128) and may fail to see that algebra may help them to make hard things easy and thus it may not convey the sense of purpose students are looking for.

Purposeful tasks and problems can be characterized as having "a meaningful outcome for the learner, in terms of an actual or virtual product, the solution of an engaging problem, or an argument or justification for a point of view" (Ainley, Bills, & Wilson, 2005, p. 194). Thus, such tasks and problems provide students with the feeling of empowerment that enable them to understand relevant situations which otherwise will remain only partially understood or totally opaque, and then to make informed decisions. Besides, engagement with appropriate tasks may stimulate a sense of intellectual fulfillment and aesthetic satisfaction for many students.

In several places in Section 1.2, we described purposeful handling of algebraic expressions according to algebraic rules. Consider, as another example, the situation inspired by a real event as shown in Figure 1.14 (Arcavi, 2008).

> The majority of the students in a class failed an examination, namely their grades were less than 50 on a 0–100 scale (0 being the lowest grade and 100 the highest). In order to improve the grades, the teacher decided to apply the following "correction factor": $f(x) = 10\sqrt{x}$ (where x is the original grade and $f(x)$ is the improved grade after the correction is applied). Thus, if a student originally got a grade of 64, his improved grade would be $10\sqrt{64} = 80$.

FIGURE 1.14 The improvement of grades situation.

After becoming acquainted with some more examples of the correction factor (e.g. 81 will be improved to 90), this authentic situation (which actually happened in a real classroom) opens up several questions for the students to explore. Since this situation relates to school life, it is quite likely that students can formulate by themselves some questions to explore.

In Figure 1.15, some of these questions are listed alongside possible approaches to answer them.

This example illustrates a real student-life situation in which "the crucial point is the power of algebra to gain insight into something that you could not do without it" (Brown & Drouhard, 2004, p. 40). Such "visible (and meaningful) algebra" (Giménez & Lins, 1996, p. 9) is not frequent in the classroom experiences of students.

Algebraic situations detached from students' lives can also be designed to be sufficiently appealing, so that engaging with them may lead students to experience victory over an intellectual obstacle and thus the engagement itself can be fulfilling. This may provide a similar sense of purpose to the one experienced by people engaged with hobbies—namely the engagement itself is the purpose (Arcavi, 2008). For this to be the case, adequate tasks and enriching classroom discussions are crucial.

18 Algebra—Setting the Scene

Possible questions	Approaches to answers
Does this correction factor leave any grades unaffected?	Solve $10\sqrt{x} = x$
Does this correction factor improve the grades of *all* students, or are there grades that will increase?	Find if there is any grade such that $10\sqrt{x} < x$
Is the correction "fair" (namely, do weaker grades gain more than strong grades)?	Explore the graph of the function $g(x) = 10\sqrt{x} < x$
How does the given correction compare to $h(x) = \frac{100+x}{2}$ (the arithmetic mean of the top possible grade and the actual grade)?	• Compare $h(x)$ with $f(x)$ algebraically or graphically. • Compare the values of the arithmetic and the geometric mean of two numbers.
Create a correction factor that you prefer and explain how you did it and why you prefer it.	Experimentation with numbers and algebraic expressions to capture desired characteristics.
Consider how the seldom-used identity function $I(x) = x$ can be helpful in solving this problem.	Describe the meaning of $I(x)$ in this situation.

FIGURE 1.15 Questions and approaches to answers on the improvement of grades.

Ideally, students who have encountered problems which convey a sense of purpose or intellectual fulfillment "come out of (algebra classrooms) armed with a new understanding of mathematics and with a new understanding of themselves as leaders, participants and learners" (Moses & Cobb, 2001, p. 17), and possibly will no longer wonder why students should learn algebra.

A different kind of answer to the question of why to learn algebra lies in developing the capability to critique the uses, misuses and abuses of mathematical arguments that can be exploited to intimidate others. By means of an unintelligible concatenation of symbols, some arguments can be wrapped with scientific respectability and thus paralyze unprepared interlocutors (afraid of challenging an algebra based argument) in order to "convince" them on the basis of hard to refute "evidence." Thus, knowledge of algebra may be crucial for, among other things, the inspection, understanding and development of a critical appraisal of the large amount of information and arguments with which we are often confronted. Following an argument (algebraic or other) and detecting its potential fallacies is both a way to strengthen thinking skills and to fence oneself off from attempts of imposing intellectual authoritarianism and even "mathematically based" propaganda.

A famous anecdote (not necessarily fully faithful to actual events) that exemplifies this is shown in Figure 1.16.

> *Diderot paid a visit to Russia at the invitation of Catherine the Second. At that time he was an atheist, or at least talked atheism ... His lively sallies on this subject much amused the Empress, and all the younger part of her Court. But some of the older courtiers suggested that it was hardly prudent to allow such unreserved exhibitions. The Empress thought so too, but did not like to muzzle her guest by an express prohibition: so a plot was contrived. The scorner was informed that an eminent mathematician had an algebraic proof of the existence of God, which he would communicate before the whole Court, if agreeable. Diderot gladly consented. The mathematician ... was Euler. He came to Diderot, with the gravest air, and in a tone of perfect conviction said, "Monsieur, $\frac{a+b^n}{n}$ = x donc Dieu existe; respondez!" ("Monsieur, $\frac{a+b^n}{n}$ = x, whence God exists; answer that!") Diderot, to whom algebra was Hebrew, ... and whom we may suppose to have expected some verbal argument of alleged algebraical closeness, was disconcerted; while peals of laughter sounded on all sides. Next day he asked permission to return to France, which was granted (De Morgan, 1915, p. 339).*

FIGURE 1.16 First example of abusing algebra.

In more recent times, Koblitz (1984) provided several examples of misuses of algebra (e.g. by creating equations relating quantities that cannot always be measured and assigned numerical values), and concludes that "whether ... arguments are used for fair ends or foul, a well-educated person should be able to approach such devices critically" (p. 253) in order to avoid using algebra (and other mathematical fields) as a source of power "to mystify and intimidate, rather than to enlighten" (p. 254). From this perspective, knowledge of algebra can be considered as a way to enhance and preserve democracy since "a successful democracy is conceivable only when and where individuals are able to "think for themselves," "judge independently," and discriminate between good and bad information" (Orrill, 2001, p. xiv).

1.4 Chapter Summary

This chapter starts to address a problématique (Section 1.1): the centrality of algebra in mathematics curricula all over the world in contrast with the many difficulties that learning it presents for students, and the subsequent reluctance to study it. We do so by posing two main questions: what is the essence of the algebra taught at school (Section 1.2) and why is it taught (Section 1.3)? We propose answers to both and provide examples to support and illustrate the arguments. Revisiting and exemplifying the nature of the subject matter (algebra's aims, actions and entities) as well as its educational value and the plausible reasons to study it, is a first step to attempt to resolve the problématique for the benefit of students, teachers and curriculum designers. The chapter also includes tasks and activities for exploration and discussion to further unpack and clarify the issues (Section 1.5).

1.5 Thinking Further

Section 1.2 Algebra—Aims, Actions, and Entities

1. Discuss with colleagues the appropriateness of the list of aims of algebra (Section 1.2.1) for evaluating a textbook, in the light of an eventual decision on its adoption. Is the list helpful, exhaustive, informative? If not, please elaborate your own.
2. Prove the Mediant Inequality: $\frac{a}{b} < \frac{c}{d} (a,b,c,d > 0) \frac{a}{b} < \frac{a+c}{b+d} < \frac{c}{d}$ (Subsection 1.2.1—Proving Theorems) in two different ways: symbolically, and graphically by representing the fraction $\frac{a}{b}$ as the ordered pair (b, a) in the Cartesian coordinate plane. Discuss with your colleagues (and possibly with your students) the advantages or disadvantages of the symbolic versus the graphical approaches to the proof of this inequality.
3. Collect examples of arithmetical calculations which can be done easily using algebra, in a similar way as the examples presented in Section 1.2.1—Calculating.
4. Solve the matches problem (Section 1.2.2) in at least three different ways. Discuss the possible pedagogical advantages of using this problem (or similar problems in which different ways of counting yield different equivalent expressions) to teach the topic of equivalent expressions. For a detailed discussion of this problem, see Hershkowitz, Arcavi, and Bruckheimer (2001).
5. A solution strategy for the quartic equation $x^2 + \left(\frac{x}{x+1}\right)^2 = 1$ was presented in Subsection 1.2.2—Handling Algebraic Expressions. The strategy consists of identifying a "formal target" (in this case, $(a - b)^2$) which helped rearranging the expressions in order to convert the equation into a quadratic. Collect or create problems in which this strategy may be useful (see, for example, the subsection "Formal targets" in Arcavi, 1994, p. 29).
6. Discuss the advantages and disadvantages of the symbolic and the graphical ways to answer the question "What do all the linear functions of the form $f(x) = ax + a$, have in common?" and how these solutions may be brought to a classroom.
7. Experience the action related to connecting representations by exploring features of the Parallel Axes Representation (PAR) presented above. For example:
    o In the Cartesian plane, the rate of change of the linear function can be envisioned by the steepness of the line that represents the function. How can the rate of change of a linear function be envisioned in the PAR? (Hint: beware, each mapping segment may be seen as having a "slope," however …)
    o Show that for (almost all) linear functions, the mapping segments (or their extensions) intersect in a single point, called the focus. Find for which linear functions the focus does not exist. Explore the possible locations of the foci in the PAR plane (to the left of the x-axis, in between the axes,

to the right of the y-axis, on the axes). What is comparable to the locations of the foci in the symbolic and graphical Cartesian representations of a linear function?
- Explore how a and b in $f(x) = ax + b$ determine the location of the foci in PAR.
- Use this exploration to reflect on the insights one may gain by connecting different representations in general and by comparing PAR with Cartesian representation of linear functions.

For a detailed exploration of the PAR for linear functions see Arcavi and Nachmias (1993).

8. Create algebraic expressions that satisfy the following conditions, and discuss with colleagues their potential for classroom use.
    - The substitution of any negative number in the expression yields a positive number.
    - The substitution of any number in the expression yields a number which is smaller than the number substituted.
    - The substitution of any number in the expression yields a number larger than 5.

9. A student was surprised to notice that $\frac{1}{2} - \frac{1}{3} = \frac{1}{2} \times \frac{1}{3}$ and he wanted to know whether there are other pairs of numbers for which their difference equals their product. Explore this task and consider the following as potential issues for discussion with colleagues and students that arise during or after the exploration:
    - Can you at first sight exclude pairs, or single numbers that you know right away will not be candidates for this property to hold?
    - Which kinds of algebraic expressions can be created in order to explore when does this property hold?
    - Consider applying the notion of function (and its graphical representations) in the exploration, and what insights, if any, may it offer in the search for a solution?

10. Discuss with your colleagues the potential difficulties and advantages of attempting to define variables and equations (and the subtleties therein) with your students. You may experience yourself or with colleagues the exercise of attempting to define variable and equation. You may find it useful to replicate the exercise of describing variable or equation using just one word (a variable is a _____) and then defining it with a whole sentence, as described in Schoenfeld and Arcavi (1988).

Section 1.3 Why Algebra?

11. The following are some quotes from students taken from Purplemath Forums (2003–2012).
    I don't need algebra, because I'm not going to college
    I won't need this stuff for my job

I really will not need algebra for "real life"
Consider the extent to which the arguments proposed in Section 1.3 may provide satisfying answers to these (or other related) students' concerns. Propose your own arguments and discuss them with colleagues and with your students.

12. Explore with your students the correction factor problem along the lines suggested in Figure 1.15. Discuss whether this problem may convey a sense of purpose for algebra.
13. Discuss with your colleagues the possibility of bringing the extract on abuses of algebra (Figures 1.16) to students and the potential influence it might have. Perhaps letting your students read it and comment on may be worth a try.
14. Select a unit or a series of tasks and problems from your favorite algebra textbook. Discuss the extent to which they convey a "sense of purpose" for algebra. Elaborate the nuances of the construct "sense of purpose" (for whom? what purpose? what would be possible antonyms of purposefulness in the context of learning algebra?). Suggestion: browse through the study conducted by Project 2061 (2013).

1.6 References

Ainley, J., Bills, L., & Wilson, K. (2005). Designing spreadsheet-based tasks for purposeful algebra. *International Journal of Computers for Mathematical Learning, 10*(3), 191–215.

Arcavi, A. (1994). Symbol sense: Informal sense-making in formal mathematics. *For the Learning of Mathematics, 14*(3), 24–35.

Arcavi, A. (2008). Algebra: Purpose and empowerment. In C. E. Greenes (Ed.), *Algebra and Algebraic Thinking in School Mathematics* (pp. 37–49). Reston, VA: NCTM.

Arcavi, A., & Nachmias, R. (1989). Re-exploring familiar concepts with a new representation. *Proceedings of the 13th International Conference on the Psychology of Mathematics Education (PME 13), Volume 1* (pp. 77–84). Paris: PME.

Arcavi, A., & Nachmias, R. (1993). What is your family name, Ms. Function? – Exploring families of functions with a non-conventional representation. *Journal of Computers in Mathematics and Science Teaching, 12*, 315–329.

Bednarz, N., Kieran, C., & Lee, L. (1996). *Approaches to Algebra: Perspectives for Research and Teaching*. Dordrecht, Boston: Kluwer Academic Publishers.

Brown, I. & Drouhard, J. P. (2004). Responses to the "Core of Algebra." In K. Stacey, H. Chick, & M. Kendal (Eds.), *The Future of the Teaching and Learning of Algebra – The 12th ICMI Study* (pp. 31–40). Boston, Dordrecht, New York, London: Kluwer Academic Publishers.

De Guzmán, M. (1995). *Para Pensar Mejor. Desarrollo de la Creatividad a Través de los Procesos Matemáticos*. Madrid: Pirámide S.A.

De Morgan, A. (1915). *A Budget of Paradoxes. Vol. 1*. (Second Edition edited by David Eugene Smith). Chicago, London: The Open Court Publishing Co.

Dictionary.reference.com (2012). *Algebra*. Definition 1. Collins English Dictionary – Complete & Unabridged Digital Edition. http://dictionary.reference.com/browse/linear+algebra (accessed September 11, 2015).

diSessa, A., Hammer, D., & Sherin, B. (1991). Inventing graphing: Meta-representational expertise in children. *Journal of Mathematical Behavior, 10*, 117–160.

Drijvers, P., Goddijn, A., & Kindt, M. (2011). Algebra education: Exploring topics and themes. In P. Drijvers (Ed.), *Secondary Algebra Education. Revisiting Topics and Themes and Exploring the Unknown* (pp. 5–26). Rotterdam, Boston, Taipei: Sense Publishers.

Encyclopedia of Mathematics (2014). Equation. www.encyclopediaofmath.org/index.php/Equation (accessed September 11, 2015).

Farrell, M. A., & Ranucci, E. R. (1973). On the occasional incompatibility of algebra and geometry. *Mathematics Teacher, 66*, 491–497.

Free Dictionary (2003–2015) http://encyclopedia2.thefreedictionary.com/Equation+(mathematics) (accessed September 11, 2015).

Freudenthal, H. (1977). What is algebra and what has it been in history? *Archive for History of Exact Sciences*, 189–200.

Freudenthal, H. (1983). *Didactical Phenomenology of Mathematical Structures* (p. 469). Dordrecht, the Netherlands: Reidel.

Friedlander, A., & Arcavi, A. (2012). How to practice it: An integrated approach to algebraic skills. *Mathematics Teacher, 105*(8), 608–614.

Gibson, J. (n.d.). *Why Learn Algebra?* www.mathgoodies.com/articles/why_learn_algebra.html (accessed September 11, 2015).

Giménez, J., & Lins, R. (1996). *Arithmetic and Algebra Instruction. Searching for the Future.* Catalonia: Copisteria Asturias.

Hershkowitz, A., Arcavi, A., & Bruckheimer, M. (2001). Reflections on the status and nature of visual reasoning – The case of the matches. *International Journal of Mathematical Education in Science and Technology, 32*(2), 255–265.

House, P.A. (1988). Reshaping school algebra: Why and how? In A. F. Coxford & A. P. Shultz (Eds.), *The Ideas of Algebra, K-12, NCTM 1988 Yearbook* (pp. 1–7). Reston, VA: NCTM.

Kieran, C. (1992). The learning and teaching of school algebra. In D. A. Grouws (Ed.), *Handbook of Research on Mathematics Teaching and Learning* (pp. 390–419). New York: Macmillan.

Kieran, C. (2004). The core of algebra: Reflection on its main activities. In K. Stacey, H. Chick, & M. Kendal (Eds.), *The Future of the Teaching and Learning of Algebra – The 12th ICMI Study* (pp. 21–34). Boston, Dordrecht, New York, London: Kluwer Academic Publishers.

Koblitz, N. (1984). Mathematics as propaganda. In D. M. Campbell & J. C. Higgins (Eds.), *Mathematics. People. Problems. Results*, Vol. III (pp. 248–254). Belmont: Wadsworth International.

Küchemann, D. (1981). Algebra. In K. M. Hart (Ed.), *Children's Understanding of Mathematics, 11–16* (pp. 102–119). Oxford, London: Alden Press.

Lins, R. C. (2011). The production of meaning for algebra: A perspective based on a theoretical model of semantic fields. In R. Sutherland, T. Rojano, A. Bell, and R. Lins (Eds.), *Perspectives on Algebra* (pp. 37–60). Dordrecht: Kluwer.

MacGregor, M., & Stacey, K. (1993). Cognitive models underlying students' formulation of simple linear equations. *Journal for Research in Mathematics Education, 24*, 217–232.

Mac Lane, S., & Birkhoff, G. (1967). *Algebra.* New York: MacMillan.

Malle, G. (1993). *Didaktische Probleme der Elementaren Algebra.* Braunschweig, Wiesbaden: Vieweg.

Moses, R. P., & Cobb, C. E. (2001). *Radical Equations: Math Literacy and Civil Right.* Beacon Press.

Online Etymology Dictionary (2001–2015). www.etymonline.com/ (accessed September 11, 2015).

Orrill, R. (2001) Mathematics, numeracy and democracy. In L. A. Steen (Ed.), *Mathematics and Democracy. The Case of Quantitative Literacy*. National Council on Education and the Disciplines (NCED) (pp. xiii–xx).

Project 2061 (2013). www.project2061.org/publications/textbook/algebra/summary/criteria.htm (accessed September 11, 2015).

Purplemath Forums (2003–2012). *Why Do I Have to Take Algebra?* www.purplemath.com/modules/why_math.htm (accessed September 11, 2015).

Schoenfeld, A. H., & Arcavi, A. (1988). On the meaning of variable. *Mathematics Teacher, 81*, 420–427.

Sherzer, L. (1973). McKay's Theorem. *Mathematics Teacher, 66*, 229–230.

Tall, D., & Thomas, M. (1991). Encouraging versatile thinking in algebra using the computer. *Educational Studies in Mathematics, 22*, 125–147.

Teachscape (n.d.). *The Broken Calculator.* http://seeingmath.concord.org/broken_calculator/ (accessed September 11, 2015).

Usiskin, Z. (1988). Conceptions of school algebra and uses of variables. In A. F. Coxford & A. P. Shulte (Eds.), *The Ideas of Algebra, K-12* (Yearbook) (pp. 8–19). Reston: NCTM.

Wagner, S. (1983). What are these things called variables? *Mathematics Teacher, 76*, 474–479.

Wikipedia, Algebra. http://en.wikipedia.org/wiki/Algebra/ (accessed September 11, 2015).

Wikipedia, Equation. http://en.wikipedia.org/wiki/Equation (accessed September 11, 2015).

Wolfram MathWorld (1999–2015). *Equation.* http://mathworld.wolfram.com/search/?query=equation&x=0&y=0 (accessed September 11, 2015).

2
SOME LESSONS FROM HISTORY

> I am sure no subject loses more than mathematics by any attempt to dissociate it from its history.
>
> (Glaisher, 1890, p. 467)

2.1 Introduction

Algebra and algebraic symbolism as we know them today are 500 years old at most. In comparison, Euclidean geometry is at least 2300 years old. The question of why geometry developed so much earlier than formal algebra is a matter of historical inquiry. However, tracing of the roots of algebra prior to the development of its symbolism can be quite enlightening for mathematics education. In this chapter, we present a few snapshots from the fascinating evolution of algebra and we suggest some lessons to be drawn from them for educational practice. These snapshots include examples from:

- Egyptian arithmetic, on the way in which problems (which nowadays we would consider word problems to be solved by means of linear equations) were approached and solved (Section 2.2);
- Babylonian mathematics, on arithmetic ways to solve some quadratic equations (Section 2.3);
- Arabic mathematics, on geometric ways to solve certain quadratic equations (Section 2.4);
- European mathematics, on the beginnings of modern symbolism and the role of negative numbers in algebra (Section 2.5).

This chapter is not to be taken as a historical account of the evolution of algebra as we know it today and as it appears in many historical treatises (e.g. Boyer, 1985;

26 Some Lessons From History

Klein, 1968; Nesselman, 1842). Rather, it illustrates episodes from which we as teachers, teacher educators, curriculum developers, and researchers may gain some insights into the nature of algebra itself, and which may have implications for algebra education.

2.2 Linear Equations in Ancient Egypt

As described in Subsection 1.2.3, equation is a central entity of algebra. As we saw, a general definition of equation refers to a statement relating two mathematical expressions (including single numbers) by means of the equals sign. The characterization of equations need not explicitly require the expression relating quantities to be symbolic, and thus such an expression can be formulated verbally and yet be considered an "equation." For example, the following sentence "*a quantity whose seventh part is added to it becomes 19*" relates 19 to a sum of an unknown and a certain part of it, and invites a search for the unknown quantity that makes the relation true. Nowadays, with our sophisticated, concise and effective symbol system we can find the solution by deciding to call the unknown quantity x, expressing the conditions of the problem using an equation ($x + \frac{1}{7}x = 19$), and then applying routine procedures to find that $x = 16\frac{5}{8}$. Once we have mastered algebraic notations and procedures, we take the symbolism for granted and may fail to appreciate how subtle and sophisticated it is. We also may not be aware that although the statement of the problem is almost 3600 years old, the above representation ($x + \frac{1}{7}x = 19$) to solve it is only about 400 years old. The problem is taken from the Rhind Papyrus (Problem #24), one of the oldest extant mathematical texts dated approximately to 1650 BCE. The Papyrus bears the name of Alexander Henry Rhind, a Scottish antiquarian, who purchased it in 1858 in Egypt. The Papyrus, which is now in the British Museum, is "not a theoretical treatise, but a list of practical problems encountered in administrative and building works. The text contains 84 problems concerned with numerical operations, practical problem solving, and geometrical shapes" (The British Museum, n.d.). Peet (1923/1970, p. 10) explains its importance as follows:

> The outstanding feature of Egyptian mathematics is its intensely practical character ... everything is expressed in concrete terms ... The Egyptian does not speak or think of 8 as an abstract number, he thinks of 8 loaves or 8 sheep ... Perhaps it is in keeping with this attitude there is ... practically no instance of the use of general formula.

However, in spite of the practical origin of the problem, we can regard some of the problems as decontextualized exercises whose solutions can be generalized, as we see below.

Not only was the modern algebraic notation not yet available to the ancient Egyptians but also they had a very different numeration system to ours. In order to describe the solution to the equation as written in the Papyrus, we first briefly explain their numeration system and the way they performed arithmetical operations within it. In hieroglyphics, a stick stands for the number 1, and the numbers between 1 and 9 are written as aggregations of sticks. A horseshoe sign ("hobble for cattle") stands for 10, and a curly sign ("coil of rope") stands for 100, a lotus flower stands for 1,000, and a bent finger sign stands for 10,000. Figure 2.1 shows these signs and the number 19607.

∩	⟲	🪷	𓂭	𓎆𓎆𓎆𓎆
10	100	1000	10000	19607

FIGURE 2.1 The numbers 10, 100, 1000, 10000, and 19607 in hieroglyphics.

We note that this numeration system is:

1. "decimal" (base ten) in the sense that the aggregation of ten symbols representing the same value can be replaced by another single symbol;
2. "non-positional" (without place value) in the sense that if one changes the order of the symbols, the whole will still represent the same quantity, and thus there is no need for a special symbol for zero;
3. it is easy to double a number: one just has to write down the same symbols again and if ten of one kind appear they can be replaced by one single symbol of the greater value.

In mathematics education, it has often been noted that the representation influences what one can do easily with it. Consider, for example, the calculation presented in Figure 2.2 in hieroglyphics and our numeration system but with the Egyptian method:

	•	1	2801
	‖	2	5602
	‖‖	4	11204
		Total	19607

FIGURE 2.2 An example of an Egyptian calculation.

What is the calculation that has been performed here? At first sight, it is clear that there is a sum of three addends: 2801, 5602 and 11204. However, there is more here than meets the eye. The second addend is twice the first and the third is twice the second. In our notation it can be written as $2801 + 2 \times 2801 + 4 \times 2801$. In other words, the calculation being performed is 7×2801. This small experience, inspired by a historical snapshot, may prompt some interesting mathematical and meta-mathematical insights. For example:

- There is more than one way to perform a multiplication of two numbers, and our standard algorithm is just one efficient possibility. Moreover, the only knowledge needed to multiply in the Egyptian way is to double numbers and to add them.
- The previous insight may induce the following question: can any two numbers be multiplied in this way? This question is tantamount to asking whether any number can be decomposed into the sum of powers of two. The answer is yes, and this is the basis of the binary system. However, unlike the case above in which all the addends add up to one of the multiplicands, one generally has to choose among the powers of two which add up to the multiplier. When multiplying with this method, for example, 37×11, one may decide that decomposing 11 into powers of 2 is more efficient that doing it for 37. Multiplication is commutative, but this method may privilege one order over the other, as we may sometimes do with the standard algorithm.
- What arithmetic/algebraic idea is the basis of this method? The method illustrates an ingenious application of the distributive law, which is a property of the numbers themselves, and does not depend on how they are written. The distributive law is applicable within any numeration system independently of its representational features. Thus some mathematical properties may be "dressed" in different ways but their existence is independent of them.
- The algorithms/procedures for performing operations are intimately linked to the representational system within which they are performed. The representational system determines to a large extent what can be done more easily, and perhaps by extension what can and cannot be "seen" (i.e. understood). Thus handling several representations can enhance our experiences and increase our opportunities for meaningful learning.

The lessons we draw from this refer to arithmetic, but some of them also apply to algebra:

- A good representation system is very important.
- There are often several different algorithms to carry out a procedure, and in different representation systems, certain choices of algorithms can lead to faster and easier work.
- Sometimes we learn properties of the underlying mathematical objects (e.g. numbers) and sometimes we learn properties related only to the representation of these objects.

- We may see different properties from different representations, so learning multiple representations leads to better understanding.

The arithmetical procedure for multiplication discussed above was presented in order to serve as a basis to return to our original equation posed by Problem #24 from the Rhind Papyrus and to examine how it is solved there.

Figure 2.3 shows the solution process of the problem "*a quantity whose seventh part is added to it becomes 19,*" presented step by step as it appears in the Papyrus, but presented in our numeration system (see, for example, Peet, 1923/1970, p. 61).

/ 1	7
/ $\frac{1}{7}$	1
1	8
/ 2	16
$\frac{1}{2}$	4
/ $\frac{1}{4}$	2
/ $\frac{1}{8}$	1
/ 1	$2 + \frac{1}{4} + \frac{1}{8}$
/ 2	$4 + \frac{1}{2} + \frac{1}{4}$
/ 4	$9 + \frac{1}{2}$
The quantity is	$16\frac{1}{2} + \frac{1}{8}$
One seventh is	$2 + \frac{1}{4} + \frac{1}{8}$
Total	19

FIGURE 2.3 Solution of Problem #24 of the Rhind Papyrus.

The method for solving this equation, certainly when we meet it for the first time, is cryptic and may remain so after some efforts to make sense of it. The Egyptian method involves arithmetical operations only, it is lengthy and the text does not share any justification of the general structure of the solution nor of each of the individual steps. Thus, it does not seem to resemble at all the straightforward and efficient symbolic solution method we use and teach today.

In order to decipher and understand the Egyptian solution one may proceed in several phases. A first phase consists of parsing the text by identifying the different solution steps, which are apparent as shown in Figure 2.4.

The second phase consists of observing each step in turn in order to understand the operations performed: on the basis of what one knows about the Egyptian arithmetic (as shown above), it is helpful to verbalize and/or rewrite the operations in our numeration system. Thus, the first step seems to be the multiplication $\left(1+\frac{1}{7}\right)\times 7$ or, in the original wording of the problem, the quantity 7 to which its seventh part is added yields 8. The second step is the multiplication $\left(2+\frac{1}{4}+\frac{1}{8}\right)\times 8$, and its result is 19. The third step is the multiplication $\left(2+\frac{1}{4}+\frac{1}{8}\right)\times 7$ and its result is $16\frac{5}{8}$ which is the number sought. Although it seems that we made some progress with the deciphering process, it still remains to understand how the pieces paste together in order to explain not only what was done but also why.

In attempt to paste the pieces together, we first notice what would seem to be the application of the conditions of the problem to a quantity of our choice and to obtain a result. The trial quantity chosen is 7, apparently because it is easy to calculate its seventh. However, the obtained result of adding one-seventh to the quantity is not 19, but 8. The second step (see Figure 2.4), although it is displayed as multiplication, can be also seen as "How many times 8 goes into 19?" and the answer is $2+\frac{1}{4}+\frac{1}{8}$. The third step consists of multiplying the obtained number (the

First Step		Second Step		Third Step		Check	
/ 1	7	1	8	/ 1	$2+\frac{1}{4}+\frac{1}{8}$	$16\frac{1}{2}+\frac{1}{8}$	
$/\frac{1}{7}$	1	/ 2	16	/ 2	$4+\frac{1}{2}+\frac{1}{4}$	$2+\frac{1}{4}+\frac{1}{8}$	
		$\frac{1}{2}$	4	/ 4	$9+\frac{1}{2}$	19	
		$/\frac{1}{4}$	2				
		$/\frac{1}{8}$	1				

FIGURE 2.4 Steps of the solution of Problem #24 of the Rhind Papyrus.

number of times that 8 goes into 19) by the initial trial quantity. In short the operation, performed is $\frac{19}{8} \times 7$. This operation is identical to the one which would result from solving $x + \frac{1}{7}x = 19$, using our algebraic methods. However, this operation results from a different conceptual process, in which the main idea underlying the concatenation of steps is proportion. Let's review the whole process in that light: after applying the conditions of the problem to 7 to obtain 8, we then look for the ratio between that result (8) and the desired result (19), namely how many times "8 goes into 19," and then we adjust our initial choice (7), since this result should be the number of times that out trial number "goes into" the unknown we look for.

There are several lessons one may learn from this process of solving equations. As in the case of multiplication, we realize how the absence or the presence of a certain representation strongly influences the way in which one carries out procedures and solves problems. In particular, we have a renewed opportunity to think about the characteristics of algebraic symbolism. On the one hand, we can appreciate the elegance and power of the algebraic symbolism which we take so much for granted and which simplifies the ways in which we solve equations nowadays. On the other hand, by virtue of its power, algebraic symbols allow us to proceed quickly and efficiently and by doing so we may engage in the luxury of forgetting the meanings of each of the steps we carry out. It can be argued that, similarly, when one masters the Egyptian method it may also allow us to forget the meaning of our actions. However, the procedure requires the invocation and the operational application of the idea of proportionality, its relations to the operations being carried out and its intrinsic relation with linear equations of the form $ax = b$.

By engaging with the exercise of describing and explaining the Egyptian method, teachers may gain another pedagogical moral. Teachers often confront the situation of trying to understand idiosyncratic ideas and partial ways of students' understanding of certain concepts. This requires the ability to analyze, unpack and even adopt the "other's perspective" in order to understand it and its sources (Arcavi & Isoda, 2007). We propose that this ability can be developed and exercised through reading and understanding historical sources of the kind described above.

2.3 Quadratic Equations in Ancient Babylonia

The mathematics that evolved in Mesopotamia between approximately 2000 BCE and 300 CE is usually called Babylonian mathematics. The numeration system used was sexagesimal (base 60, but with 10 as a sub-base), and numerals were written as marks on clay tablets using basically two symbols only: ⊤ to represent units and ⟨ to represent tens. Thus, for example, the combination of symbols ⟨⊤⊤⊤ represents 23. We do not describe here in detail the characteristics of the Babylonian numeration system and its ambiguities.

In Babylonian mathematics, we find what some historians call "rectangular equations" (e.g. Gandz, 1937). The following is one example: "*the sum of the sides of a rectangle is 29 and its area is 210, find the side lengths.*" The phrase "sum of the sides" refers

32 Some Lessons From History

to the sum of the two side lengths, not the full perimeter. Today we could represent this problem with the pair of equations ($xy = 210$ and $x + y = 29$), substitute one variable and solve the resulting quadratic equation to obtain the solution $x = 14$ and $y = 15$ (or $x = 15$ and $y = 14$). Figure 2.5 shows the way in which the Babylonians solved it (according to Van der Waerden, 1954, p. 64) as expressed in our modern notation.

> Take one half of 29, which is 14.5
> $14.5 \times 14.5 = 210.25$
> $210.25 - 210 = 0.25$
> The square root of 0.25 is 0.5
> $14.5 + 0.5 = 15$ (the length)
> $14.5 - 0.5 = 14$ (the width)

FIGURE 2.5 Solution to the quadratic problem in ancient Babylonia.

Such a solution is puzzling at first sight, and one possible way to make sense of it (and also to check for the generality of the method) is to translate it into algebraic symbolism. Two possible ways to interpret (anachronistically) the above solution with the aid of algebra are shown in Figure 2.6.

Babylonian method (in decimal notation)	First interpretation (with algebraic symbols)	Second interpretation (with algebraic symbols)
Take half of 29 (14.5)	$x + y = 29$ It is legitimate, although unusual, to consider $x = 14.5 + c$ and thus $y = 29 - (14.5 + c) = 14.5 - c$	$x + y = 29$ $\dfrac{x+y}{2} = \dfrac{29}{2}$
$14.5 \times 14.5 = 210.25$	–	$\left(\dfrac{x+y}{2}\right)^2 = 210.25$
$210.25 - 210 = 0.25$	$(14.5 + c)(14.5 - c) = 210$ $210.25 - c^2 = 210$ $c^2 = 210.25 - 210 = 0.25$	$\left(\dfrac{x+y}{2}\right)^2 - xy = 210.25 - 210$ $\left(\dfrac{x-y}{2}\right)^2 = 0.25$
The square root of 0.25 is 0.5	$c = 0.25$	$\dfrac{x-y}{2} = 0.5$
$14.5 + 0.5 = 15$ (the length)	$14.5 + c = x$ Because $c = x - 14.5$	$\dfrac{x+y}{2} + \dfrac{x-y}{2} = 14.5 + 0.5 = 15$
$14.5 - 0.5 = 14$ (the width)	$14.5 - c = y$ Because $c = 14.5 - x$	$\dfrac{x+y}{2} - \dfrac{x-y}{2} = 14.5 - 0.5 = 14$

FIGURE 2.6 Solution to the quadratic problem from ancient Babylonia using algebra.

The first interpretation can be generalized as follows:

$xy = a$

$x + y = b$

We can write $x = \dfrac{b}{2} + c$ and thus $y = \dfrac{b}{2} - c$

thus $\left(\dfrac{b}{2} + c\right)\left(\dfrac{b}{2} - c\right) = a$

$\dfrac{b^2}{4} - c^2 = a$

$c^2 = \dfrac{b^2}{4} - a$

$c = \sqrt{\dfrac{b^2}{4} - a}$

Hence $x = \dfrac{b}{2} + \sqrt{\dfrac{b^2}{4} - a}$ and $y = \dfrac{b}{2} - \sqrt{\dfrac{b^2}{4} - a}$

The second interpretation leads to the same generalization.

As we will discuss later on in this chapter, we do not claim that this is the way that Babylonians discovered the solution to this problem. As we have seen, the written record of their solution is numerical, without any symbolism. We also do not discuss how they arrived at their solution methods, nor whether they were aware of, or concerned with, generality. What we would like to draw from this example is the way in which algebra serves **us** well to make sense of numerical methods and to show their generality. As such, history provides us with a bountiful source of nice problems (see, for example, Swetz, 1989), with inspiring solution methods that may enrich our repertoire of alternative solutions, and with opportunities to compare and contrast them.

2.4 A Geometric View of Algebra From Arabic Mathematics

In the second half of the 8th century and the 9th century CE scientific and cultural activity flourished in the Baghdad Caliphate. Muhammad ibn Musa al-Khwarizmi (the name is spelled differently in different sources) was one of the famous mathematicians of this period. Little is known about his life, but his work is well known, as mentioned in Chapter 1. In the following, we quote some extracts from the English version by Karpinski (1915) of al-Khwarizmi's most famous book, which in itself is a translation and an adaptation from the Latin version of the original Arabic. The extracts illustrate two main characteristics of the algebra in the book: it resorts to geometry for solving quadratic equations and it is syncopated

34 Some Lessons From History

(Nesselman, 1842), namely equations are written in words and contractions of words including some symbols.

"The following is an example of squares equal to roots: a square is equal to five roots. The root of the square then is 5, and 25 forms its square" (Karpinski, 1915, p. 69). In our modern notation, the "root" refers to the length of the square (which we will label x) and the "square" means its area (numerical values without units). So the statement can be expressed as $x^2 = 5x$, $x = 5$. In this case, since the referent is geometrical (and negative numbers were not developed at the time), the second root (–5) is not mentioned. In the chapter entitled "Concerning roots and numbers equal to a square" (Karpinski, 1915, p. 71) the following famous problem is presented (see Figure 2.7).

CHAPTER IV

Concerning squares and roots equal to numbers

The following is an example of squares and roots equal to numbers: a square and 10 roots are equal to 39 units. The question therefore in this type of equation is about as follows: what is the square which combined with ten of its roots will give a sum total of 39? The manner of solving this type of equation is to take one-half of the roots just mentioned. Now the roots in the problem before us are 10. Therefore take 5, which multiplied by itself gives 25, an amount which you add to 39, giving 64.

FIGURE 2.7 A famous problem from al-Khwarizmi (as it appears in Karpinski, 1915, p. 71).

The equation $x^2 + 10x = 39$ is solved by literally "completing the square," that is, by drawing a square of unknown side length and then applying the conditions of the problem (for example, annexing to it two identical rectangles with one side of length 5 and the other with the same length as the side of the square), as shown in Figure 2.8 (ibid., pp. 81, 83).

This problem and its geometrical solution are well known and are often used in classrooms in order to visualize both the process of completing a square and the solution of a specific quadratic equation. Less well known is an example in which al-Khwarizmi solves an equation which has two distinct positive solutions, and thus neither can be ignored in the geometrical method. Consider the equation $x^2 + 21 = 10x$ which has two solutions $x = 3$ and $x = 7$. The original extract is shown in Figure 2.9 (Karpinski, 1915, pp. 86–87, footnotes from the original were omitted).

The process described above is presented with its geometrical equivalent, as follows (the way in which geometrical figures are denoted is faithful to this source—note that sometimes the conjunction of two letters denote an area and sometimes a length, later on a rectangle is labeled by means of four letters).

The first construction is a square (denoted *ab*) to represent x^2 to which a rectangle of area 21 is annexed (such that one of its sides is of length x), as shown in Figure 2.10.

Another method also of demonstrating the same is given in this manner: to the square *a b* representing the square of the unknown we add ten roots and then take half of these roots, giving 5. From this we construct two areas added to two sides of the square figure *a b*. These again are called *a g* and *b d*. The breadth of each is equal to the breadth of one side of the square *a b* and each length is equal to 5. We have now to complete the square by the product of 5 and 5, which, representing the half of the roots, we add to the two sides of the first square figure, which represents the second power of the unknown. Whence it now appears that the two areas which we joined to the two sides, representing ten roots, together with the first square, representing x^2, equals 39. Furthermore it is evident that the area of the larger or whole square is formed by the addition of the product of 5 by 5. This square is completed and for its completion 25 is added to 39. The sum total is 64. Now we take the square root of this, representing one side of the larger square and then we subtract from it the equal of that which we added, namely 5. Three remains, which proves to be one side of the square *a b*, that is, one root of the proposed x^2. Therefore three is the root of this x^2, and x^2 is 9.

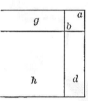

FIG. 5. — Incomplete figure. From the Dresden manuscript.

FIG. 6. — From the Dresden manuscript.

FIGURE 2.8 Solution of al-Khwarizmi's famous problem (as it appears in Karpinski, 1915, p. 81).

CHAPTER V

Concerning squares and numbers equal to roots

The following is an illustration of this type: a square and 21 units equal 10 roots. The rule for the investigation of this type of equation is as follows: what is the square which is such that when you add 21 units the sum total equals 10 roots of that square? The solution of this type of problem is obtained in the following manner. You take first one-half of the roots, giving in this instance 5, which multiplied by itself gives 25. From 25 subtract the 21 units to which we have just referred in connection with the squares. This gives 4, of which you extract the square root, which is 2. From the half of the roots, or 5, you take 2 away, and 3 remains, constituting one root of this square which itself is, of course, 9.

If you wish you may add to the half of the roots, namely 5, the same 2 which you have just subtracted from the half of the roots. This give 7, which stands for one root of the square, and 49 completes the square.

FIGURE 2.9 A second problem from al-Khwarizmi (as it appears in Karpinski, 1915, p. 75).

FIGURE 2.10 First step of the solution to the second problem.

The length *hd* of the combined figure is 10 (since its area is the area of the square combined with the area of the rectangle, and in the problem it is given that the total area is 10 roots, that is 10*x*).

We proceed to bisect the length *hd* at point *e* (*he* = *ed*), draw a perpendicular to *hd* at point *e* to obtain the midpoint *t* of *ag*, as shown in Figure 2.11.

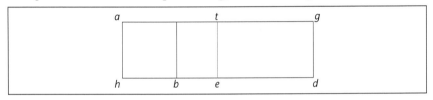

FIGURE 2.11 Second step of the solution to al-Khwarizmi's second problem.

We extend *te* to point *c* such that *tc* = *tg*. In such a way, we obtain the square *tgcl* of area 25 as shown in Figure 2.12.

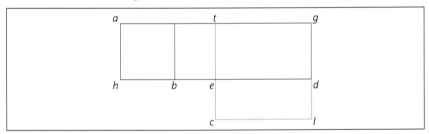

FIGURE 2.12 Third step of the solution to al-Khwarizmi's second problem.

We now form within the rectangle *ecdl* the square *ecnm* (see Figure 2.13).

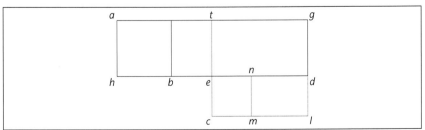

FIGURE 2.13 Fourth step of the solution to al-Khwarizmi's second problem.

It can be shown that $dl = eb$, and $lm = te$, thus the area of the rectangle $ndlm$ is equal to the area of the rectangle with b, t, and e as three of its vertices. The area of the square $encm$ is $25 - 21 = 4$, and its side is 2. This implies that the side ah of the original square is 3. This geometrical construction assumed that the "root" (the value of x) is less than 5, but a similar construction can be made assuming it is greater than 5, and thus the other root becomes $5 + 2 = 7$. For the corresponding figure that illustrates this solution see Task 10 in Section 2.6.

The geometrical solution is intricate and less straightforward than the efficient algebraic algorithm to solve the given quadratic equation. However, it is enlightening to see how the geometrical construction illustrates the solution process and how the two solutions 3 and 7 emerge from it.

2.5 Beyond Solving Equations: The Emergence of Algebra in Europe

2.5.1 Some Algebraic Rules and Their Explanation

Due to his contributions to the development of algebra as we know it today, the mathematician François Viète (1540–1603), or Franciscus Vieta in the Latin spelling, is considered by many historians as the "true founder of modern mathematics" (e.g. Klein, 1968, p. 5). He studied law and most of his adult life worked in the public service devoting his spare time to mathematics. His most important work *In Artem Analyticem Isagoge* (Introduction to the Analytic Art) appeared in 1591.

The following extracts deal with elementary rules of algebra, and provide the flavor for the algebra in which symbols and (abbreviated) words were mixed as a way of writing (called syncopated, see Nesselman, 1842) and for the kind of explanations underlying these rules. Consider, for example, the following algebraic rules: $A - (B + D) = A - B - D$ and $A - (B - D) = A - B + D$. Pause for a moment, and think about the repertoire of explanations available to us as teachers to justify these equalities. The explanations provided by Vieta as they appear in Klein (1968, pp. 331–332) are as follows: when a sum is to be subtracted from a quantity (first case), each of its addends can be subtracted separately. However, when a difference is to be subtracted from a quantity (second case), the result will be to subtract the minuend of the difference and to add its subtrahend (see Figure 2.14).

It is worth noticing that the operations deal with "quantities" and that negative numbers were not fully established as legitimate mathematical entities at the time this text was written. A testimony to that in this text is evidenced by the subtraction. This is discussed insofar as one takes away a smaller quantity from a larger one. It is also worth noticing that in this text the operations and the equality are expressed in words, and there are no brackets to prioritize the performance of certain operations over others (another example of the syncopated character of the text). However, the role of the brackets is indeed described in the case of $A - (B + D)$ as the magnitude to be subtracted "is conjoined with some magnitude."

> **Vieta's *Analytic Art***
> **Precept II**
>
> Let there be two magnitudes A and B, and let the former be greater than the latter. It is required to subtract the less from the greater. ... subtraction may be fittingly effected ... and disjoined, they will be A "minus" B, ...
>
> Nor it will be done differently if the magnitude which is subtracted is itself conjoined with some magnitude, since the whole and the parts are not to be judged by separate laws; thus, if "B 'plus' D" is to be subtracted from A, the remainder will be "A 'minus' B, 'minus' D," the magnitudes B and D having been subtracted one by one.
>
> But if D is already subtracted from B and "B 'minus' D" is to be subtracted from A, the result will be "A 'minus' B 'plus' D," because in the subtraction of the whole magnitude B that which is subtracted exceeds by the magnitude D what was to have been subtracted. Therefore, it must be made up by the addition of that magnitude D.

FIGURE 2.14 Vieta's explanations for $A - (B + D) = A - B - D$ and $A - (B - D) = A - B + D$.

The justification for the rule $A - (B + D) = A - B - D$ is that "the whole and the parts are not to be judged by separate laws," namely, if one subtracts a whole $(B + D)$ one should subtract each of its parts B and D. In the case of $A - (B - D) = A - B + D$, the justification states that by subtracting B, too much has been taken away since we are to subtract less than B. How much more was taken away? Precisely D, and thus it should be added in order to compensate.

It is interesting to contrast this sense-making explanation with the ways we may encounter in classes today. Certainly, explanations will vary according to the textbook, the level of the students and the educational context. Sometimes this sense-making explanation is presented in modern language. Sometimes these rules may be presented formally without any explanation. In other cases, perhaps the number line serves as a means to illustrate it. Yet another way to present this states that a (–) sign before the brackets is tantamount to multiplication by –1.

2.5.2 Negative Numbers

As mentioned above, the full incorporation of negative numbers into mathematics is only about four centuries old. Yet, as recently as the beginnings of the 19th century there was opposition to their incorporation as legitimate mathematical objects. Although this opposition is a historical curiosity, it is worth discussing for its potential pedagogical benefits.

One of the most vocal oppositionists was William Frend (1757–1841), an Englishman who was a rebel in more senses than one and who was banished from Cambridge where he had been a tutor. The salient feature of his book entitled *The Principles of Algebra*, published in 1796, is Frend's stark opposition of the use of negative numbers in mathematics. Figures 2.15, 2.16 and 2.17 show three of his arguments.

> ...an attempt is made to explain the nature of negative numbers, by allusions to book-debts and other arts. Now, when a person cannot explain the principles of a science without reference to metaphor, the probability is, that he has never thought accurately upon the subject.

FIGURE 2.15 Frend's first argument against negative numbers (1796, p. 4).

> A number may be greater or less than another number; it may be added to, taken from, multiplied into, and divided by another number; but in other respects it is very untractable: though the whole world should be destroyed, one will be one, and three will be three; and no art whatever can change their nature. You may put a mark before one, which it will obey: it submits to be taken away from another number greater than itself, but to attempt to take it away from a number less than itself is ridiculous. Yet this is attempted by algebraists, who talk of a number less than nothing, of multiplying a negative number into a negative number and thus producing a positive number, of a number being imaginary.

FIGURE 2.16 Frend's second argument against negative numbers (1796, p. 4).

> ... the mark − before f denotes that it is to be taken away from some number which is not written down, and we cannot make any sense of the expression $-f$.

FIGURE 2.17 Frend's third argument against negative numbers.

In Section 2.7 Task 11, there are several arguments proposed for discussion in order to counter Frend's contentions. Regardless of whether we include negative numbers under the label of algebra or not, their rejection affects the way in which algebra is done. The following is an example of how Frend solves a quadratic equation avoiding negative roots. This may have been one of the reasons why the famous mathematician Augustus De Morgan (1806–1871), who was Frend's son-in-law, described Frend's ideas as "anti-algebraical" (De Morgan, 1915, Vol. 1, p. 197). The term "anti-algebraical" refers to the impediment of treating all possible cases in a general way.

40 Some Lessons From History

$$\text{Let } x + \sqrt{5x+10} = 8.$$

(a) $\therefore \sqrt{5x+10} = 8 - x$
(b) $\therefore 5x + 10 = 64 - 16x + x^2.$
$\therefore 5x + 16x - x^2 = 64 - 10$
(c) $\therefore 21x - x^2 = 54$
(d) $\therefore \dfrac{441}{4} - 21x + x^2 = \dfrac{441}{4} - 54 = \dfrac{441-216}{4} = \dfrac{225}{4}$

$$\therefore \sqrt{\dfrac{441}{4} - 21x + x^2} = \sqrt{\dfrac{225}{4}}$$

$$\dfrac{21}{2} - x = \dfrac{15}{2}$$

$$\therefore x = \dfrac{21}{2} - \dfrac{15}{2} = \dfrac{6}{2} = 3.$$

In this cafe the root $x - \dfrac{21}{2}$ cannot be ufed; for, by the conditions of the queftion, x is lefs than eight.

FIGURE 2.18 A solution to a quadratic equation avoiding negative numbers (Frend, 1796, p. 111).

It is interesting to scrutinize Frend's algebraic arguments to see how he avoids negative numbers. Consider, for example, the step from (c) to (d) in Figure 2.18. He subtracts (c) from 441/4, which is a standard way of completing the square. In this step, he uses the rule $A - (B - D) = A - B + D$. As we saw, this rule can be applied without any need to resort to negative numbers, provided that $A > B$, and $B > D$ (which is the case here, since $\dfrac{441}{4} > 54$. It is worth noticing that the non-recognition of negative numbers implies that in the initial equation $x + \sqrt{5x+10} = 8$, both addends (x and $\sqrt{5x+10}$) must be positive and less than 8. Thus, as Frend writes towards the end of the paragraph, he cannot allow $x - \dfrac{21}{2}$ as a square root of the completed square because it would be negative. Admitting this option ($x - \dfrac{21}{2} = \dfrac{15}{2}$) leads to the second root ($x = 18$). Interestingly, we would also reject this root because it does not satisfy the original equation $x + \sqrt{5x+10} = 8$, since the symbol $\sqrt{}$ is taken to mean the positive root only. So, where does the 18 arise? In line (b) of the solution in Figure 2.18, where both sides of the equation of line (a) have been squared, not only $\sqrt{5x+10} = 8 - x$ leads to line 3, but also $\sqrt{5x+10} = x - 8$ (for which 18 is a solution). However, if the original problem posed by Frend had started at (c) with the equation $21x - x^2 = 54$ (in which the constraint $x < 8$ is no longer in effect), both roots would have been admissible, since both are positive and also no step of the argument makes explicit or implicit use of negative numbers.

Frend's solution to this equation illustrates how the inclusion of negative numbers has enabled us to achieve general and simpler methods, instead of considering many particular cases (when trying to avoid negative numbers).

2.6 Chapter Summary

The modest account of some episodes from the history of mathematics in this chapter is a very brief presentation of snapshots without any pretention of comprehensiveness. Moreover, when relying on the history of mathematics to pursue goals of mathematics education, we run the serious risk of committing the historiographical wrongdoing called Whig history (Fried, 2001). This mistreatment of history consists of looking into the past with the hindsight of the present, at the risk of distorting the original spirit of the ideas by imposing on them our present knowledge, tools and biases.

One way of minimizing "Whiggism" is to present, as far as possible, original (or semi-original) sources to attempt to create non-mediated encounters with ideas from the past, and whenever possible noting what we do today, and how different it may be. Thus we can resort to the history of algebra to inspire us and to teach us. Here is a summary of what we propose can be derived from the account presented as well as from the suggestions below for thinking further (see Section 2.7).

- Whereas our present way of doing algebra has only been developed during the last 400 years, some of the problems we solve at school today (or the type of problems) are very ancient. This is especially the case with equation solving.
- The tools used to solve problems in the past are elaborate and ingenious; we can follow them, understand them and relate the solution methods to some central mathematical concepts (such as proportions). Sometimes this understanding is easiest for us using today's symbolism, but we should be careful not to attribute this way of thinking to the source we are deciphering.
- Representations (e.g. systems to write numbers, thinking of unknowns as lengths, etc.) are human creations, and as such may differ radically from one another. Moreover, the characteristics of a representation or a notation system have a strong influence on the way one performs operations and on the strategies one applies to solve problems.
- We take algebraic symbolism as we know it today for granted. However, history provides us with a perspective to appreciate its efficiency, its conciseness and the power it provides us in order to solve classes of problems at once, which otherwise would have to be considered separately.
- History can enlarge our repertoire of problems, solution strategies and ways of explaining them.
- History can show us how some ideas we now take so much for granted in algebra instruction took a long time to develop and even were opposed by scholars until not very long ago. Such opposition is worth knowing and discussing with students, whose difficulties sometimes may mirror difficulties in history.
- Mathematical treatments of some algebraic topics evolve and the ways some problems were addressed in education in the past have disappeared altogether (e.g. variations of the Egyptian methods known as the Rule of False Position

which was still being studied in the 19th century, see Section 2.7, tasks 6 and 7) in favor of more algebraic methods. This strengthens the imperative for wide opportunities for all students to access algebra and learn it.
- There are many and varied connections between algebra and geometry. They allow us to both enrich our set of problem solving strategies and to make sense of algebraic symbolism in certain situations. We have illustrated this with the methods for solving quadratic equations, but there are other instances as well (e.g. the distributive law, squaring a binomial).
- Deciphering what looks like cryptic mathematical texts requires strategies such as parsing the text (i.e. dividing it into pieces), making sense of the operations performed, attempting to paste the pieces into a coherent whole and the like. As teachers, we may experience a similar process when trying to find the coherence and structure behind some of the cryptic arguments, strategies or solutions proposed to us by students.

2.7 Thinking Further

Section 2.2 Linear Equations in Ancient Egypt

1. Perform the multiplication 29×19 using the Egyptian method (in our numeration system).
2. Solve variations of Problem #24 of the Rhind Papyrus ("a quantity whose seventh part is added to it becomes 19"). For example, replace the seventh part by a fourteenth part.
3. Figure 2.19 shows the solution process of Problem #25 of the Rhind Papyrus, as it appears in Peet (1923/1970, pp. 61–62). Express in words and in algebraic symbolism the problem that is being solved and explain the solution process.
4. Can equations of the form $ax + b = c$ be solved by the Egyptian method? Explain.
5. In an account of the work of the mathematician Vieta (François Viète, 1540–1603) and his great contributions to the development of modern algebra, it is written:

> Viète noted that in problems involving the "cosa" or unknown quantity ... instead of reasoning from it is known to what was to be demonstrated, algebraists invariably reasoned from the assumption that the unknown was given and deduced a necessary conclusion from which the unknown can be determined.
>
> (Boyer, 1985, p. 336)

In his famous book *How to Solve it*, the mathematician Georg Polya (1887–1985) describes a problem solving strategy called "working backwards" as follows: "assume what is sought as already found" (Polya, 1973, p. 227). Discuss the similarities between Boyer's statement about Vieta and Polya's statement and discuss the way these statements depict the process of solving algebraic equations.

Some Lessons From History   **43**

1	2
$\frac{1}{2}$	1
—	—
/ 1	3
2	6
/ 4	12
$\frac{2}{3}$	2
/ $\frac{1}{3}$	1
—	—
1	$5\frac{1}{3}$
/ 2	$10\frac{2}{3}$
—	—
The quantity is	$10\frac{2}{3}$
A half is	$5\frac{1}{3}$
Total	16

FIGURE 2.19 Solution to Problem #25 of the Rhind Papyrus.

6. "The Rule of False Position, Single and Double, is a method of solving equations of the first degree in one unknown by guessing the answer and then adjusting the guess in terms of the conditions of the problem" (Sanford, 1951, p. 307). This rule was in use until the 19th century, and the Egyptian solution method is the earliest known example of the "single" version of the rule. Figure 2.20 shows an extract from Keith (1822, pp. 225–227), in which he describes and exemplifies the Rule of Double False Position to solve a word problem. Read the extract which includes the rule and its application to an example. In the solution to the example, some blank spaces have been left for you to fill using the rule.

DOUBLE POSITION.

Definition. By *Double Position*, or two suppositions, are solved those questions wherein the errors are proportional to the difference between the true number, and each supposition.

RULE.

Suppose any two convenient numbers, and proceed with them according to the nature of the question, marking the errors (with + or —) according as they exceed or fall short of the truth.

Then,

Multiply the first supposition by the second error, and the second supposition by the first error, and divide the sum of the products by the sum of the errors, if they are differently marked; or the difference of the products by the difference of the errors, if they are marked alike, and the quotient will be the nnmber sought.

Examples

What number is that, which, being multiplied by 3, the product increased by 4, and that sum divided by 8, the quotient may be 32?

Suppose 12	Again, suppose 108
×	× ....
....	....
+	+ ....
....	....
Divided by 8	Divided by 8
....	....
But it should be 32, so the error is −27	But it should be 32, so the error is +9

By the rule

1st supposition   12   −27

2nd supposition   108   +9

....
Answer 84

FIGURE 2.20 Solution of a problem using the Rule of Double False Position.

(a) Fill the blanks in Figure 2.20 and find the solution to the problem.
(b) Solve the problem by algebra.
(c) Try to solve this problem by another method other than algebra or the Rule of False Position. For example, consider a method from Section 3.7.

7. As a result of the development of algebraic symbolism, the Rule of False Position (single or double) appeared less and less, even though there are still texts in the 19th century, like Keith (1822) quoted above, which teach the

Some Lessons From History 45

rule (without explanation). Today, the Rule of False Position is almost unknown except in books on the history of mathematics, but the tenacity of this method can be judged from the fact that Perry (1899, p. 25) had to argue to replace it by algebra as late as 1899 (see Figure 2.21). Following Perry's comment, justify the Rule of False Position algebraically.

> Those parts of arithmetic called "Equation of Payments," "Barter," "Profit and Loss," "Fellowship," "Alligation" of many kinds, "Position," "Double Position," Conjoined Proportion," and many other, are, when we strip them of their technical terms and artificial complexities, the simplest of algebraic exercises, and they ought to be treated as such.

FIGURE 2.21 Perry's extract on the Rule of False Position.

8. A mother shares all the sweets she has between her three daughters as follows: the first gets half of what she has plus two sweets, the second gets half of the remainder plus two sweets, and the third gets half of what is now left plus two sweets. How many sweets did she have altogether? Solve this problem by three methods: the Rule of False Position, algebra, and any other method of your choice.

Section 2.4 A Geometric View of Algebra From Arabic Mathematics

9. Provide an alternative geometrical representation (in the same style of al-Khwarizmi) to the solution process described in Figure 2.7.
10. In Section 2.4, we describe al-Khwarizmi's solution to the problem "a square and 21 units equal to 10 roots." The diagram for the first root ($x = 3$) of this equation is constructed step by step and explained (see Figures 2.9, 2.10, 2.11, 2.12 and 2.13). Figure 2.22 is the diagram (unlettered) for obtaining the second root ($x = 7$). Add the corresponding letters and explain it.

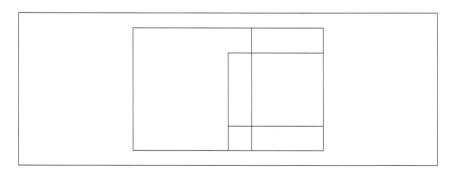

FIGURE 2.22 Diagram for finding the second root of $x^2 + 21 = 10x$.

Section 2.5 Beyond Solving Equations: The Emergence of Algebra in Europe

11. Identify the following ideas in Frend's arguments against negative numbers, as expressed in the original source provided above:
    - The explanations of negative numbers rely on examples from outside mathematics.
    - The "−" sign makes sense as long as it relates to subtracting a small number from a larger one; it does not make sense as a mark before a number.
    - Suppose these arguments are being raised by one of your students. What would you reply to them, and in general to the opposition to admit negative numbers?

    Figure 2.23 shows an extract from Whitehead (1911, pp. 82–83). Alfred North Whitehead (1861–1947) made notable contributions to the foundations and philosophy of mathematics. Examine how this extract can be considered a reply to Frend's opposition, and to what extent this argument can be discussed with students.

What is the use of all this elaboration? At this point our friend, the practical man, will surely step in and insist on sweeping away all these silly cobwebs of the brain. The answer is that what the mathematician is seeking is Generality. This is an idea worthy to be placed beside the notions of the Variable and of Form so far as concerns its importance in governing mathematical procedure. Any limitation whatsoever upon the generality of theorems, or of proofs, or of interpretation is abhorrent to the mathematical instinct. …

Let us see how generality is gained by the introduction of this idea of operations. Take the equation $x + 1 = 3$; the solution is $x = 2$. Here we can interpret our symbols as mere numbers, and the recourse to "operations" is entirely unnecessary.

But, if x is a mere number, the equation $x + 3 = 1$ is nonsense. For x should be the number of things which remain when you have taken 3 things away from 1 thing; and no such procedure is possible. At this point our idea of algebraic form steps in, itself only generalization under another aspect. We consider, therefore, the general equation of the same form as $x + 1 = 3$. This equation is $x + a = b$, and its solution is $x = b - a$. Here our difficulties become acute; for this form can only be used for the numerical interpretation so long as b is greater than a, and we cannot say without qualification that a and b may be any constants. In other words we have introduced a limitation on the variability of the "constants" a and b, which we must drag like a chain throughout all our reasoning. Really prolonged mathematical investigations would be impossible under such conditions. Every equation would at last be buried under a pile of limitations. But if we now interpret our symbols as "operations," all limitation vanishes like magic. The equation $x + 1 = 3$ gives $x = +2$, the equation $x + 3 = 1$ gives $x = -2$, the equation $x + a = b$ gives $x = b - a$ which is an operation of addition or subtraction as the case may be. We need never decide whether $b - a$ represents the operation of addition or of subtraction, for the rules of procedure with the symbols are the same in either case.

FIGURE 2.23 A possible reply by Whitehead to Frend's arguments.

2.8 References

Arcavi, A., & Isoda, M. (2007). Learning to listen: From historical sources to classroom practice. *Educational Studies in Mathematics, 66*(2), 111–129.

Boyer, C. B. (1985). *A History of Mathematics*. Princeton, NJ: Princeton University Press.

De Morgan, A. (1915). *A Budget of Paradoxes. Vol. 1*. (Second Edition edited by David Eugene Smith). Chicago, London: The Open Court Publishing Co.

Frend, W. (1796). *The Principles of Algebra*. London: J. Davis. Also available at http://books.google.co.il/books?id=6VsUAAAAQAAJ&printsec=frontcover&source=gbs_ge_summary_r&cad=0#v=onepage&q&f=false (accessed September 11, 2015).

Fried, M. N. (2001). Can mathematics education and history of mathematics coexist? *Science and Education, 10*(4), 391–408.

Gandz, S. (1937). The origin and development of the quadratic equations in Babylonian, Greek and early Arabic algebra. *Osiris, 3*(2), 405–557.

Glaisher, J. W. L. (1890). Presidential Address at the British Association for the Advancement of Science. *Nature 42* (1089), 464–468.

Karpinski, L. C. (1915). *Robert of Chester's Latin Translation of the Algebra of Al-Khowarizmi*. London: MacMillan and Co. Ltd. Also available at https://archive.org/details/robertofchesters00khuw and at www.wilbourhall.org/pdfs/mbp/robertofchesters00khuw.pdf (accessed September 11, 2015).

Keith, T. (1822). *The Complete Practical Arithmetician: Containing New and Useful Improvements Adapted to the Use of Schools and Private Tuition*. Eight Edition, London. Also available at: http://books.google.co.il/books?id=cf82AAAAMAAJ&printsec=frontcover&hl=iw&source=gbs_ge_summary_r&cad=0#v=onepage&q&f=false (accessed September 11, 2015).

Klein, J. (1968). *Greek Mathematical Thought and the Origin of Algebra* (Translated by Eva Brann). Cambridge, MA: M.I.T. Press.

Nesselman, G. H. F. (1842). *Versuch einer kristischen geschichte ser algebra, 1 Teil. Die Algebra der Griechen* [Essay on a critical history of algebra, 1st Part. The algebra of the Greeks]. Berlin: G Reimer.

Peet, T. E. (1923). *The Rhind Mathematical Papyrus: British Museum 10057 and 10058*. The University Press of Liverpool Ltd. and London: Hodder & Stoughton Ltd. (Nendeln, Liechtenstein: Kraus Reprint 1970).

Perry, J. (1899). *Practical Mathematics. Six Lectures delivered to Working Men*. London: Her Majesty's Stationery Office.

Polya, G. (1973). *How to Solve it*. Princeton, NJ: Princeton University Press (Second printing).

Sanford, V. (1951). The rule of false position. *Mathematics Teacher, 44*(5), 307–309.

Swetz, F. J. (1989). Using problems from the history of mathematics in classroom instruction. *Mathematics Teacher, 82*(5), 371–376.

The British Museum (n.d.). *Rhind Mathematical Papyrus*. Retrieved from www.britishmuseum.org/explore/highlights/highlight_objects/aes/r/rhind_mathematical_papyrus.aspx (accessed September 11, 2015).

Van der Waerden, B. L. (1954). *Science Awakening*. Groningen, Holland: Noordhoff, Ltd.

Whitehead, A.N. (1911). *An Introduction to Mathematics* (pp. 82–83). London: Williams and Norgate. Also available at www.gutenberg.org/files/41568/41568-pdf.pdf (pp. 62–63) (accessed September 11, 2015).

3

SEEING ALGEBRA THROUGH THE EYES OF A LEARNER

> If one is truly to succeed in leading a person to a specific place, one must first and foremost take care to find him where he is and begin there. This is the secret in the entire art of helping.
>
> (Kierkegaard, 1859/1998, p. 45)

> The facts of nature are what they are, but we can only view them through the spectacles of our mind.
>
> (Gould, 1991, p. 264)

3.1 Introduction—Putting on Teachers' Bifocal Spectacles

This chapter aims to show teachers something of what algebra looks like to its learners. In doing this we will analyze where the challenges of algebra are, demonstrate how some of the thinking that serves students well before they learn algebra needs to be considerably reoriented in order to make progress and identify the resources and creativity that students can bring to their learning.

Teachers need to combine knowledge of mathematics with insights into the psychology of thinking and learning, in order to see the learner's perspective and to take advantage of this to improve lessons.

As we learn, we build up new conceptual structures (or as some prefer to say, we adopt new discourses) through which we see, interpret and describe the world. A simple example is children's changing idea of "big." They begin by establishing an undifferentiated quality of bigness; even babies will often choose the largest piece of food. Things that are long, or tall, or heavy, or large in volume or area are all simply "big." Later, when ideas separating length, area, volume, and mass are in place, these differentiated concepts of being big are automatically imposed on perceptions of the world and children no longer see things just as big, but automatically see the length or weight or area.

It is similar with learning algebra. An aim of algebra education is that learners will automatically see the world through the lens of algebra, whenever this is helpful. For example, successful students can think of income tax payable as a function of taxable income. They may envisage a graph of tax against income, and see the marginal tax rate (e.g. 20 cents in the dollar) as the slope of the graph. They may consider qualitatively or quantitatively how the rate of change of the function changes as income rises and the implications of this for personal behavior and in society. These underlying ideas can influence understanding even though citizens never do any algebraic manipulations in relation to their tax. The point is not that people should "do algebra" to understand their tax, but that an outcome of a good algebra education is that fundamental algebraic concepts (such as functions) can be brought to bear on situations encountered in life. As students progress through life and education, it is as if they are progressively putting new lenses in the spectacles through which they see the world. And these new lenses, in this case for seeing mathematics and algebra in particular, cannot be taken off, to go back to an earlier stage. They are put on permanently, even if they sometimes get cloudy over time.

Teachers already wear the spectacles of a mathematically capable adult and this presents a major problem, because they need at the same time to see the world through the eyes of their students. This means that they have to wear two pairs of lenses at once – their own adult lenses (which they cannot take off) and other lenses matching as closely as possible those of their learners. This chapter aims to give teachers some bifocal spectacles, with both adult lenses and learner lenses, to help them see the world of algebra through the eyes of their learners. By knowing how their students see the world, teachers can better help those students to put on and learn to use algebra spectacles to the full. These bifocal spectacles are part of what is called teachers' pedagogical content knowledge, a notion that will be further addressed in Section 4.1.

The fundamental message of the chapter, illustrated with many examples, is that algebra is a new way of thinking that requires substantial change for students. Knowledge of how students think about algebra can inform algebra education and can help teaching (Stacey, Chick, & Kendal, 2004). In Section 3.2, the ideas about symbolism that students bring to algebra are discussed. In Section 3.3, the process–object dilemma is introduced and some implications are explored. Section 3.4 discusses how young students see the equals sign, and why this affects their algebra learning. Section 3.5 discusses the slippery concept of mathematical structure and the role of expressions, numeric and algebraic, in capturing it and revealing hidden aspects. Section 3.6 reviews how fundamental patterns of thinking that students develop through learning arithmetic need to be changed to use algebra to solve problems. A strong understanding of numbers and arithmetic is an essential foundation for learning algebra, but the transition to algebra requires considerable reorientation of ideas. Section 3.7 explores the various methods that are available for solving equations, again discussing how practices developed through previous learning need to be refined. In Section 3.8, there is a return to the process–object dilemma, this time as it affects more advanced learners developing ideas about functions. The chapter concludes with problems and tasks for thinking further. Appreciating student thinking can influence the teaching of algebra and teachers' interactions with students, and this chapter gives some suggestions. However, broad questions of algebra curriculum and teaching programs are left to Chapter 4.

3.2 What Do Algebraic Letters Represent?

For nearly everyone, the defining feature of algebra is its use of letters from the Latin alphabet. When students come to learn algebra, they bring assumptions about algebraic letters that come from their previous experiences with the alphabet, especially if their native language uses Latin letters. Some students new to algebra answered these two questions (MacGregor & Stacey, 1997):

1. David is 10 cm taller than Con. Con is h cm tall. What can you write for David's height?
2. Sue weighs 1 kg less than Chris. Chris weighs y kg. What can you write for Sue's weight?

What sort of responses do students give? Of course, many responses are correct ($10 + h$ and $y - 1$ and variations) but there are many other answers. Commonly, students omit the operation sign, responding with $10h$, $h10$ or $1y$. Some responses use letters standing for relevant words like D (David), Dh (David's height), or Uw (unknown weight) or include equations such as $h = h + 10$ where h is used to vaguely indicate height (David's, Con's, maybe other people's) rather than a precisely defined variable. Other students think about the alphabet, giving responses like x (the letter one before y) or 24 (because y is the 25th letter) for Sue's weight, and r (10 letters after h) or 18 (h is the 8th letter, and 18 is 10 more) for David's height. Alphabetically based responses like these are most common with beginning students, but unfortunately, variants are also often seen from students who have been learning algebra for some years. Other students choose a numerical value for h or y giving answers like 110 cm for David's height. When the real situation is not a guide for choosing numerical values, the value of 1 is often assigned to a letter, perhaps because students are often told that an algebraic letter such as x by itself without a coefficient means $1x$, which they interpret as meaning one of a x unit.

Examining these responses demonstrates how students begin to make sense of algebra using their old spectacles, drawing on their previous experience of letters and numbers. All students have used initial letters before as shorthand to stand for a word, and so they often bring this to their understanding of algebra. Students may deduce that the position in the alphabet is important, especially if they have played with codes (e.g. the number–letter cipher replacing letters by numbers a = 1, b = 2 etc) or solved popular puzzles such as finding words that "cost a dollar" (i.e. where the sum of the letter positions is equal to 100). The "Ask Dr. Math" mathematical question website (The Math Forum, n.d.) gives a list of "dollar words" from "abatements" (where 1+2+1+20+5+13+5+14+20+19=100) through "mailboxes" to "writing." Some number systems, although not those discussed in Chapter 2, also use letters in alphabetical order as numerals. For example, the ancient Greeks used the first ten letters of their alphabet as the digits for 1 to 10 (Boyer, 1968) as does modern Hebrew. These ideas can be seen in students' initial thinking about algebra.

Teachers who understand that these prior understandings are likely to interfere with learning algebra can help their students by directly discussing the differences between the world of codes and other notation systems and the world of algebra. They can stress that alphabetic position is unimportant and that many other fundamental aspects of using letters also do not apply in algebra; that different letters can stand for the same number but that a letter has only one numerical value within a problem (Küchemann, 1981; Steinle, Gvozdenko, Price, Stacey, & Pierce, 2009); that using initial letters such as h for height can be a useful mnemonic device but is not necessary and it is not height in general that is being signified but one specific height so that the answer $h = h + 10$ does not describe the relationship between two heights. Another key point to stress is that algebra is not a shorthand where we jot down mathematical ideas in a quick abbreviated way. Algebraic notation is indeed wonderfully compact "shorthand," but it only works if you follow strict rules about what the letters stand for and how to write them in meaningful combinations. As MacGregor and Stacey (1997, p. 15) point out:

> Students beginning algebra base their initial interpretations of letters and algebraic expressions on intuition and guessing, on analogies with other symbol systems they know, or on a false foundation created by misleading teaching materials. They are often unaware of the general consistency of mathematical notation and the power that this provides.

A basic tenet of teaching is to start with what the students already know. Students' prior knowledge assists learning by providing mental hooks on which to build new concepts. However, the discussion above and some of the sections below show that prior knowledge can also thwart new learning when there are unaddressed conflicts between the new and the old in students' minds.

3.2.1 Fruit Salad Algebra—Misleading Teaching With Long-Term Consequences

Teachers often use the idea that algebra is a type of shorthand in their explanations. This has some historical roots. Section 2.5.1 explained how modern algebraic symbolism began as "syncopated algebra" using a mix of symbols and abbreviated words. It is also a useful aid to memory—in the formula $A = \pi r^2$ it is very good that the letters A and r are the numerical values of the area and radius respectively. However, this idea of algebraic letters as abbreviations causes problems. In some countries "fruit salad algebra" (MacGregor, 1986) is a popular introduction to algebra. Indeed it has been popular for many years, as the extract from Joseph Ray's

1886 textbook in Figure 3.1 shows. In fruit salad algebra students learn to simplify expressions such as $5a + 2b - 3a + b = 2a + 3b$ by thinking that "5 apples and 2 bananas take away 3 apples and then add another banana" results in 2 apples and 3 bananas. Similarly they might explain that $3(2c + 5d) = 6c + 15d$ by observing that 3 groups of 2 cats and 5 dogs contain 6 cats and 15 dogs altogether. Even when the physical objects are not fruit, this is still "fruit salad algebra," falsely teaching that letters in algebra stand for physical objects rather than numbers (e.g. the number of objects involved). It avoids considering the invisible multiplication signs (e.g. that $5a$ is really the product of two numbers $5 \times a$) and the important properties of multiplication that make these simplifications possible. Fruit salad algebra makes simplifying some algebraic expressions seductively easy, but it is not really doing algebra at all. It is better to avoid using instructional techniques with a wrong message, no matter how effective they seem to be in the short-term. Learning to see through the new spectacles of algebra is much more important than quick success in manipulation.

This "letter-as-object" misconception can haunt students in their efforts to set up equations throughout their algebra careers. Evidence of this has been available for many years (e.g. Küchemann, 1981). Consider the two multiple choice items in Figure 3.2, with responses from 964 Australian students from Grades 7 to 9 to one of the algebra tests in an online assessment system (Stacey et al., n.d.). For the doughnut question in Figure 3.2, 24% of students were correct (d is the price of one doughnut) but the most popular answer was "doughnuts" chosen by 34% of students (reading $6d = 12$ as an abbreviated version of the sentence "6 doughnuts

ADDITION.

Art. 53. Addition in Algebra, is the process of collecting two or more algebraic quantities into one expression, called their sum.

CASE I.

When the quantities are similar, and have the same sign.

1. James has 3 pockets, each containing apples; in the first he has 3 apples, in the second 4 apples, and in third 5 apples.

In order to find how many apples he has, suppose he proceeds to find their sum in the following manner: 3 *apples,*
4 *apples,*
5 *apples,*
12 *apples.*

Suppose, however, that, instead of writing the word *apples,* he should merely use the letter *a,* thus: $3a$
$4a$
$5a$
$12a$

It is evident that the sum of 3 times *a,* 4 times *a,* and 5 times *a,* would be 12 times *a,* or $12a$, whatever *a* might represent.

FIGURE 3.1 Extract from Dr. Joseph Ray's 1886 textbook showing "fruit salad algebra" (pp. 33–34).

cost $12"). Both this answer and the answer "one doughnut" revealed the letter-as-object misconception, encouraged by fruit salad algebra teaching. In the roses question, 31% of students correctly chose $4r + 5g = 70$, 15% chose $r + g = 70$ (which they probably read as "the roses and the gardenias cost $70"), and 53% chose $10r + 6g = 70$, which they probably read as a shorthand version of the true but not necessary statement that "10 roses and 6 gardenias cost $70." About two-thirds of students have selected options which arise by thinking of the letters as standing for the physical objects, in this case roses and gardenias, rather than as the numbers of plants that have been bought. This error is also evident in the work of senior students, for example when setting up equations in linear programming. Students who cannot set up equations and expressions correctly in order to model situations are unable to capitalize on the practical value of algebra for problem solving. Because readily available digital technology can do algebraic manipulations to solve equations (see Chapter 5), it is more important for students to be able to set up equations and to correctly read the equations of others, than solve any but the simplest equations by hand. Fortunately, as demonstrated in Chapter 4, there are many good alternatives to introducing the rules of algebraic manipulation that do not rely on fruit salad algebra.

LUCY'S DOUGHNUTS

Lucy bought 6 doughnuts for $12. She wanted to work out how much each doughnut cost. She wrote the equation $6d = 12$. In Lucy's equation, d stands for:
(Alternatives: doughnuts, cost of one doughnut, number of doughnuts, one doughnut, dollars)

ROSES AND GARDENIAS

For my garden, I bought r red rose bushes and g white gardenia bushes. The roses cost $4 each. The gardenias cost $5 each. Choose the equation that says that the total cost was $70.
(Alternatives: $4r + 5g = 70$, $10r + 6g = 70$, $r + g = 70$)

FIGURE 3.2 Two multiple choice items probing understanding of letters in algebra (from Stacey, Steinle, Price, & Gvozdenko, n.d.).

3.3 The Process–Object Duality

As noted above, a very common incorrect expression for David's height is to give $h10$ or $10h$ instead of the correct $h + 10$. All but a tiny proportion of students answering this way would find David's height by addition if they were working with numbers, so they are writing $h10$ to indicate addition, not multiplication. As with the previous examples where students brought prior experiences with letters and words into algebra, some students overgeneralize their knowledge of other notation systems and conventions, where conjoining (placing one alongside the other) indicates some form of adding. For example, we write $2\frac{1}{3}$ to indicate $2+\frac{1}{3}$

rather than $2 \times \frac{1}{3}$. Indeed, putting two sets of objects physically together (conjoining) is the very simplest meaning of addition. Even our place value system indicates adding components just by putting them alongside each other (so 245 is 2 hundreds + 4 tens + 5 ones). These prior experiences often explain responses such as $h10$ or $10h$. However, very often there is something deeper than this involved in students' difficulties in writing expressions like $h + 10$.

Although arithmetic is the most important prerequisite for algebra and although algebra in its initial stages can be seen as generalized arithmetic, algebra and arithmetic have different orientations. One is that arithmetic is mostly about getting numerical answers, whereas algebra describes mathematical structures. When children are asked to do addition in arithmetic, the question (say 46 + 91) is worked on to give a single number "product," in this case the mathematical object 137. One writes 46 + 91 = 137. Given this background, many learners find it very puzzling that the "question" $h + 10$ has the "answer" $h + 10$ and the best that can be written to mimic 46 + 91 = 137 is the very unsatisfying $h + 10 = h + 10$. There is an urge to do something to indicate the addition has been done, such as writing $h10$ so that it is not left "unclosed" (Collis, 1974). Whereas 46 + 91 can be seen as prescribing a process of adding and 137 is the product of this process, $h + 10$ simultaneously signifies the process and the product. The same is true even for multiplication because a statement such as $m \times n = mn$ is just a change of notation for multiplication, although it is psychologically more acceptable since something seems to have been done. The confusion caused to early learners by the dual nature of algebraic expressions to indicate both a process and a product is often called the process–product dilemma (Kieran, 1992). In this book, in order to link with a broader theory described below, the name process–object dilemma (Sfard, 1991) is used instead. There are several other names in the literature for this widely observed phenomenon.

The tendency to "closure" driven by a need for an "answer" that looks distinct from the "question" is also evident in common false simplifications such as simplifying $2a + 5b$ as $7ab$. Küchemann (1981) found that nearly half a large sample of British 13-year-olds made this error. A follow-up survey to Küchemann's work (Hodgen, Küchemann, Brown, & Coe, 2008) thirty years later found that algebra results were broadly unchanged. They report a student who explained the wrong answer as:

> $8g$ sounds more like maths … than $8 + g$ … which sounds (like a) bit of a sum which you have to work out; but $8g$ just seems like an answer … in itself … but $8 + g$, you still think, "Oh, what will it equal?"
>
> (Hodgen et al., 2008, p. 9)

A similar item was used in the 2011 TIMSS study (Foy, Arora, & Stanco, 2013). Item M042086 (find $2a + 2b + 4$ given $a + b = 25$) had an international average of 35% correct at Grade 8. Success in this item depends on recognizing that $2a + 2b = 2(a + b)$, but also identifying the "$a + b$" as a single mathematical object (equal to 25). The low international success rate on this apparently straightforward item contrasts strongly with the considerably better 50% success rate on an item to solve two simultaneous equations, which involves many more steps. This indicates something deep is involved. Algebraic expressions simultaneously represent a process and an object, and to work with them well, a student must sometimes unpack the process that an expression signifies and at other times treat the expression as a single mathematical object. Developing and properly applying this versatile dual view of algebraic entities as objects and as processes is a key part of growing algebraic maturity.

3.4 The Meaning of the Equals Sign

Another difficulty for algebra that predisposes students to consider expressions such as $h + 10$ to be incomplete lies in limited meaning given by some students (and their teachers) to the equal sign. As noted above, in arithmetic the sign $=$ can be interpreted as a sign which links a question on the left with an answer on the right as in $46 + 91 = 137$ and gives the instruction to "work it out now" (Kieran, 1981). Especially in the first years of school, teachers often pose calculation tasks just by writing an incomplete equality, as in $46 + 91 = \_\_\_\_$, with the equals sign announcing where to put the answer. Understanding the equals sign just as a signal to do a calculation is inadequate for algebra, and indeed also for dealing with structural features of numbers and their operations. In algebra, the sign $=$ needs to be also interpreted in a relational manner as a statement of equality i.e. that the two quantities on the left and right have the same value and indeed one can replace the other. As Carpenter, Franke and Levi (2003, p. 22) note:

> A limited conception of what the equals sign means is one of the major stumbling blocks in learning algebra. Virtually all manipulations on equations require understanding that the equals sign represents a relation.

Students without this relational understanding will, for example, often reject statements such as $8 = 5 + 3$ (because 8 is the answer not the question), write a calculation such as "twice 6 plus 3" as $2 \times 6 = 12 + 3 = 15$, and fill the box in the statement $8 + 4 = \square + 5$ not with the correct 7 but with 12 or 17 (when a further 5 is added to 12 to get the "final answer"). Behr, Erlwanger, and Nichols (1980) demonstrated that many students viewed the equals sign only as "work it out now" even in the upper grades of elementary school. This situation continues in many countries, although it seems to develop more from common conventions and practices than the undue complexity of the idea. For example, Carpenter et al. (2003) have shown that young children can develop the relational view of the equals sign with appropriate instruction. They emphasize that many of the changes were not immediate or easy, but at the end of their year-long study a large majority of children from Grade 1 up dealt well with both ideas of equality. Discussion of the meaning and truth or falsity of statements such as $5 + 3 = 8$, $8 = 5 + 3$, $8 = 8$,

5 + 3 = 5 + 3, and 3 + 5 = 5 + 3 is central. Many young students initially only accept the first one as true or sensible. Knuth, Stephens, McNeil, and Alibali (2006) provide evidence that not having a relational sense of the equals sign has a large impact on success in algebra.

3.5 Algebra for Recording and Revealing Mathematical Structure

Responses to items like 8 + 4 = ☐ + 5 can also reveal aspects of students' understanding of mathematical structure. Students at a later stage of development than those giving the incorrect answers of 12 or 17 as above, can give the correct answer of 7 but they find it by calculating 8 + 4 = 12, so 12 = ☐ + 5, so ☐ = 7. With a relational understanding of equality, students can look at the equality as a whole and reason that because 5 is one more than 4 and the two sides are equal, ☐ must be one less than 8. Only these students are able to solve problems such as 569 + 294 = ☐ + 570 or 569 − 294 = 579 − ☐ efficiently. They then appreciate the equality of the two sides of the equation, and also can analyze the structure of the expression, noting, for example, that 579 is 10 more than 569, so preserving the equality will require a subtrahend that is 10 more than 294. (This property of subtraction is similar to the one justified by Vieta in Figure 2.14.) The ability to appreciate equality and analyze structure in these examples is very important to dealing successfully with algebraic expressions, which also describe structure through their "unclosed" nature.

Students' compulsion to calculate numerical answers can also make it difficult for them to see patterns and mathematical structure. Consider, for example, the pattern in Figure 3.3, which is a variation of the pattern in Figure 1.1. How many tiles are there, when the pattern is continued to more rows? It is much easier to see this by observing the pattern in the uncalculated expressions 1, 1 + 2, 1 + 2 + 3, 1 + 2 + 3 + 4, … than by looking only at the total numbers of squares 1, 3, 6, 10 … It is also easier to find the general number of corners by considering the sequence of unclosed expressions formed by adding the number of corners on each level 1 + 2 + (3 − 2), 1 + 2 + 3 + (4 − 2), 1 + 2 + 3 + 4 + (5 − 2) … than the totals 4, 8, 13, 19, …. The "unclosed" numerical expressions show the structure that is to be generalized. These numerical expressions are a precursor to algebraic expressions, which above all reflect and reveal structure.

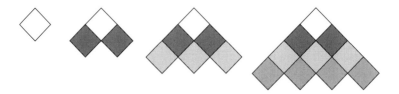

FIGURE 3.3   Growing patterns of tiles, corners, and edges.

In Japan, a high performing country in mathematics, there is a strong focus on "shiki" (mathematical expressions) as a pillar of the curriculum. Watanabe (2011) gives many examples, including a Grade 4 lesson about the problem of finding the change when items costing 140 yen and 460 yen are bought with a 1000 yen note. The aim is not to give the answer of 400 yen, but to learn to write expressions such as 1000 − (140 + 460). Activities such as this make a bridge from arithmetic to algebra and emphasize mathematical structure, an emphasis that has value well beyond algebra. Kaput, Carraher, and Blanton (2008) and Cai and Knuth (2011) provide ideas for ensuring that the early school years provide students with rich algebraic experiences.

Another key feature of algebra is that it reveals and reflects structures that are equivalent (i.e. give the same numerical outcomes) but into which different meanings can be read. Because students become very focused on carrying out the routines for manipulating algebraic expressions, they often miss the bigger picture that changing algebraic form highlights different aspects of mathematical structure and so enables different problems to be solved. For example, much of the curriculum about quadratic expressions is about changing structure. The standard form is a sum of three terms $ax^2 + bx + c$. This explicitly shows several properties such as the value when $x = 0$, whether the function has a maximum or a minimum and the "width" of the parabola of its graph. Factorizing changes the sum of terms to a product $a(x - h)(x - k)$, and this form shows the zeros of the function. Completing the square changes the sum of terms to a sum or difference of squares, which reveals other features, including the co-ordinates of the turning point of the graph. The symbolic manipulation that students learn is to find equivalent expressions, but the underlying reason for the activity is that these different structures solve different problems. Students tend to miss the purpose because of their focus on the rules.

This elusive idea of mathematical structure is also evident when interpreting algebraic expressions. A new idea for students is that algebraic answers to problems often can be read in multiple ways. Consider the following problem:

> Mark and Jan earned $\$T$ between them, but Mark earned $\$D$ more than Jan. How much does each person get?

If Mark gets $\$m$ and Jan gets $\$j$, then it is simple to set up the two equations $m + j = T$ and $m = j + D$ and find the solution $j = \frac{1}{2}(T-D)$ and $m = \frac{1}{2}(T-D) + D$. Careful reading of these expressions shows how to actually distribute the money: first give Mark his extra $\$D$ and then give each person half of the $\$(T - D)$ left over. Rearranging the expressions shows another distribution method: $j = \frac{1}{2}T - \frac{1}{2}D$ and $m = \frac{1}{2}T + \frac{1}{2}D$. To follow this distribution method, divide the total money in half, and have Jan give $\$\frac{1}{2}D$ to Mark. Arcavi (1994) describes this as finding non-equivalent meanings from equivalent expressions.

The feel for symbols and the confidence in them that guide the search for new aspects of the original meanings are part of what Arcavi (1994, 2005) calls symbol

58 Seeing Algebra Through the Eyes of a Learner

sense. Arcavi (1994) gives many more examples of symbol sense and its value for mathematical work. One important feature is looking carefully at symbols rather than jumping immediately to automatic procedures. In the next section, the power of algebra for solving very wide classes of problems in almost completely routine ways is highlighted. However, algebra with symbol sense is much more than a routine of symbol pushing.

In summary, algebraic notation captures and displays mathematical structure. Students' experiences in learning arithmetic only rarely foster an appreciation of structure. This is another of the many obstacles which students have to negotiate in order to make the transition from arithmetic to algebra. Algebra spectacles enable students to seek structure and to read the meaning of the structure expressed in the symbols.

3.6 Transitions From Learning Arithmetic to Learning Algebra

3.6.1 Contrasting Arithmetic and Algebraic Problem Solving

Singapore schools are renowned for their high achievement in mathematics. The curriculum is based around problem solving so there are some difficult problems in the highly competitive Primary School Leaving Examination (PSLE). This is undertaken by Grade 6 students and largely determines which secondary school they attend. Since formal algebra is not part of the curriculum until secondary school, students are expected to solve these problems arithmetically. Surprisingly, some tutors teach their students algebra so that they can solve some of the PSLE problems more easily. How can it be that tutors might think learning algebra is the easiest path? The answer to this puzzle lies in the contrast between the power of solving problems in arithmetic and algebra, the methods used and consequently the obstacles that students encounter. Figure 3.4 shows two PSLE problems of contrasting difficulty. The high difficulty of the sweets problem caused a controversy among parents.

STAMPS
Father gave Jason 50 stamps. 16% of them were from Australia. After Mary gave Jason some more stamps from Australia, the percentage of his stamps which were from Australia increased to 30%. How many stamps did Mary give Jason? (PSLE, quoted by Dindyal, 2006, p. 182)

JIM AND KEN
Jim bought some chocolates and gave half of them to Ken. Ken bought some sweets and gave half of them to Jim. Jim ate 12 sweets and Ken ate 18 chocolates. After that, the number of sweets and chocolates Jim had were in the ratio of 1:7 and the number of sweets and chocolates Ken had were in the ratio 1:4. How many sweets did Ken buy? (PSLE 2009, quoted by Yeap, 2010)

FIGURE 3.4 Two problems from the Singapore Primary School Leaving Examination.

How might Grade 6 students solve the stamps problem without algebra? Singapore students are taught to use the "model method" to assemble information from word problems and help the solution. In this case, a bar (see Figure 3.5) is drawn with length representing Jason's total number of stamps after Mary's gift, made up of three components. Jason's original stamps consisted of 42 from elsewhere and 8 (16%) from Australia, so these are marked on the bar, along with the unknown number of stamps from Mary. The 30% and then 70% are also marked. From this, it is reasonably easy to see that 70% is 42 stamps, so the total number of stamps is 60 and so Mary gave Jason 10 stamps. Note that in this solution we began with 50 stamps, found 16% (the original number of Australian stamps), then found the number of other stamps (42), which is 70% of the new total, then found the new total to be 60 and found the number of stamps from Mary. This demonstrates a characteristic of arithmetic solutions: they proceed as much as possible from one known number or numbers, to calculate another meaningful quantity and so on, combining information until the desired quantity is reached. The bar model provides a visual support for the solution and secondary teachers also use it to introduce algebra, by displaying the unknown quantity and the relationships.

The arithmetic solution for the sweets problem is more difficult. A suitable bar model is shown in Figure 3.6. Note that the bar cannot be fully drawn to scale, because the dimensions are not all known at the time it is drawn. The bars represent the chocolates and sweets of each person. Bars are drawn to represent the number of chocolates and sweets for each person after sharing, noting that they are equal before the eating begins. Without 12 sweets, Jim has seven times more chocolates than sweets, so Jim's chocolate bar is seven times as long as his remaining sweets bar and this is shown on the bar model. Similarly, Ken's chocolate bar, without the 18 he ate, is four times as long as his full sweets bar. So Ken's chocolate bar is made up of 18 plus 4 full sweets bar, each of which is 12 sweets plus Jim's remaining sweets. Since Ken's chocolate bar is the same length as Jim's, 18 + 4 × 12 = 66 is equal to 3 of Jim's remaining sweets bar. Consequently, Jim had 22 sweets remaining, 34 before he ate 12 and 7 × 22 = 154 chocolates. The purchases must have been 2 × 154 chocolates and 2 × 34 sweets. The bar model is extremely useful for guiding this solution. Solving the sweets problem is especially difficult because there are no definite numbers with which to start a direct chain of calculations. Instead, two quantities (lengths) which are equal are gradually

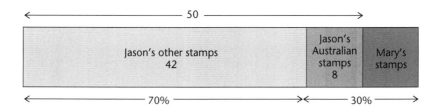

FIGURE 3.5 Likely bar model for the stamps problem in Figure 3.4.

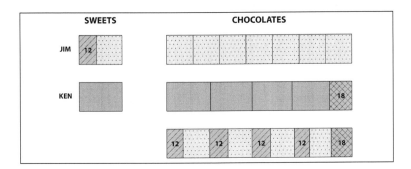

FIGURE 3.6 Bar models for the sweets PSLE problem in Figure 3.4.

uncovered and equated (the 7 unknown bar pieces [numbers of chocolates] equal to 4 of these bar pieces plus 66 chocolates) which gives the solution an algebraic character, even though no symbols are used.

Figure 3.7 shows the solutions of these problems using algebra. There are several points to note. The first is that the two problems are solved with the same overall plan. Descartes (and similarly Vieta as noted in Section 2.7 Task 5) described the plan like this:

> If, then, we wish to solve any problem, we first suppose the solution already effected, and give names to all the lines that seem needful for its construction – to those that are unknown as well as to those that are known. Then, making no distinction between known and unknown lines, we must unravel the difficulty in any way that shows most naturally the relations between these lines, until we find it possible to express a single quantity in two ways. This will constitute an equation since the terms of one of these two expressions are together equal to the terms of the other.
>
> *(Descartes, 1925, p. 6)*

In modern language the plan is as follows. Allocate an algebraic symbol to each precisely defined unknown quantity. Write down all the relationships between all the quantities, which will result in some equations. Use learned methods to solve the equations or use a computer algebra system (see Chapter 5) if they are too difficult. Interpret the answer in terms of the original problem. Of course, there are still difficulties for students, especially in identifying all the relationships and in setting up the equations. Just as with the arithmetic solution, knowledge of ratio and percentage has to be used flexibly and carefully and all of the information needs to be extracted from the problem statements. However, once mastered, the algebraic method of solving problems through equation solving is extremely powerful. It has a straightforward overall plan, and standard techniques for the solving. The challenging arithmetic puzzles faced by the PSLE candidates are routine when students are competent in algebra. Moreover, the theory of equations

STAMPS	JIM AND KEN
\multicolumn{2}{c}{**Choosing the unknowns**}
Let m be the number of stamps Mary gave to Jason.	Let x be the number of chocolates bought by Jim and let y be the number of sweets bought by Ken.
\multicolumn{2}{c}{**Setting up the equations**}
Jason has $50 + m$ stamps altogether. He has $m + 16\%$ of $50 = m + 8$ Australian stamps. Hence $m + 8 = 30\%$ of $(m + 50)$ $m + 8 = 0.3(m + 50)$	After the sharing and the eating, the number of sweets and chocolates that Jim had were in the ratio 1:7 $(y/2 - 12) : x/2 = 1:7$ The number of sweets and chocolates that Ken had were in the ratio 1:4 $y/2 : (x/2 - 18) = 1:4$, hence $7y - 168 = x$ and $4y = x - 36$
\multicolumn{2}{c}{**Solving the equations**}
$m + 8 = 0.3m + 0.3 \times 50$ $0.7m = 15 - 8 = 7$ $m = 10$	$4y = 7y - 168 - 36$ substituting in $7y - 168$ for x $3y = 168 + 36 = 204$ $y = 68$ $x = 7y - 168 = 476 - 168 = 308$
\multicolumn{2}{c}{**Interpret the answer**}
Mary gave Jason 10 stamps.	Ken bought 68 sweets and Jim bought 308 chocolates.

FIGURE 3.7   Solving the PSLE problems using algebra.

enables us to appreciate that there may be multiple or no solutions, and helps to predict how many solutions to expect. That is why equation solving is so important in the school curriculum. Algebra reduces the demand for creativity, but it opens many new doors.

On a web forum, where the difficulty of the sweets problem was discussed, there is a probably hastily typed contribution from a student who attests to the power of the routines of algebra to solve problems more easily than using arithmetic reasoning:

> The model method is a pain. just use ratio and basic algebra and there u hv [you have] it. I was in P6 last year and i solved that question in 4 minutes munching on popcorn.
>
> *(Kiasu Parents, n.d.)*

3.6.2 Fundamental Ideas of Equation Solving

The section above shows the power of equation solving. However, for most students it is not easy and students coming to equation solving for the first time have a lot to learn. They must know about algebraic notation (as discussed in Section 3.2), how to accurately express relationships between variables and the valid equation solving moves (discussed in Section 3.7), and also appreciate the power that learning the new method offers. But they also need to understand some fundamental differences between the arithmetic problem solving that they have done in the past and the new algebraic method. This is another instance where teaching is assisted by seeing algebra through the eyes of a learner, being able to put on the spectacles of the student. As Stacey and MacGregor (2000, pp. 149, 151) point out:

> at every stage of the process of solving problems by algebra, students may be deflected from the algebraic path by reverting to thinking grounded in arithmetic problem solving methods … The compulsion to calculate prevents students looking for, selecting, and naming the appropriate unknown or unknowns, and prevents them focusing on … "forward operations" in formulating an equation. It prevents some students from attempting an algebraic approach, and deflects others away from an algebraic method that they have started.

First students need to experience how an equation will be useful; they need to understand the general strategy. Sometimes students think that writing down an equation is only describing the problem, and not a step towards solving it. They are focused on working out the answer with the "backwards operations" typical of arithmetic problem solving rather than the "forwards operations" of the algebraic method. An example is provided by students' solutions to a problem about distances travelled by a bus on a 3-day tour which covered 1410 km in total. The distance travelled on Day 2 was 85 km further than on Day 1. The distance travelled on Day 3 was 125 km further than on Day 1. Students were told to let x stand for the number of kilometers travelled on Day 1 and were instructed to use algebra to work out the distance travelled each day. Stacey and MacGregor (2000) described how some good students, although asked to use algebra, did not begin with an equation like $x + (x + 85) + (x + 125) = 1410$. When asked why not, many described (although typically not in an articulate way) how they saw the equation only as a description of the problem rather than a first step to the solution. Instead their first line of working was an equation such as $x = \frac{[1410 - (85 + 125)]}{3}$ or sometimes even the very general $x = \frac{[c - (a+b)]}{3}$. These students have done all the solving work in their heads, using logical arithmetic reasoning. The equations they wrote are conceived as formulas to show how to calculate the answer from known information. This behavior has also been noted by other researchers around the world (e.g. Kieran, 1992). These students need to understand the overall strategy of solving equations, where you work on a description of the problem situation, which is itself manipulated step by step, rather than undertaking a chain of calculations of meaningful quantities which head towards a solution, as is done in arithmetic. There is a dilemma for teaching here. It is obviously sensible to solve simple problems in order to learn equation solving, but if these problems can be done easily without algebra, the value of learning algebra for equation solving is not evident. Using some harder problems is essential.

Another aspect of the transition from solving problems with arithmetic to solving problems with algebra lies in naming the unknown. This is one of the points that Descartes made in the quote above, only 400 years ago. The unknown "line" (we now think of this as a quantity) is given a name and then treated in just the same way as the known "lines" (quantities). Experts classify the stamps problem as a problem with one unknown: probably, although not necessarily, the number of stamps that Mary gives. However, beginning students see many unknowns in this problem (how many Mary gave, how many Jason then had, how many of those were Australian, etc.). Sometimes they give all of these unknowns their own algebraic symbols, and sometimes they give some or all of them the same symbol. For example, the number of Australian stamps that Jason had before and after Mary's gift might erroneously be given the same symbol, resulting in equations like $x = x + m$. In algebraic problem solving, an unknown must be a precisely specified quantity: it is not just anything that is not known. Whereas arithmetic problem solving proceeds by targeting one meaningful quantity that is unknown (e.g. the number of stamps Jason had at the start), then finding its numerical value, then moving onto the next unknown quantity until the answer is reached, in algebra "the unknown(s)" need to be precisely defined at the beginning.

A summary of some key transition points for solving problems using algebra is given in Figure 3.8. Each row describes a fundamental feature of solutions which rely on logically reasoning just about numbers on the left and the algebra idea is given on the right. Each of these transitions is a point at which students may face conceptual or strategic difficulties.

Solving a problem with arithmetic	Solving a problem with algebra
Operating with and on known quantities to calculate unknown quantities.	Operating with and on known and unknown quantities.
Solution proceeds along a chain of successive calculations, working progressively towards the answer.	Solution proceeds along a chain of logically linked equalities or inequalities.
Unknowns transient, representing intermediate stages of calculation.	Unknown(s) identified and stable throughout the problem.
Equation (if any) is interpreted as a formula for calculating answers or narrative of what happened to a number.	Equation interpreted as formula, narrative or a description of relationships between quantities.
Intermediate quantities have a ready interpretation.	Intermediate quantities may not have a ready interpretation.

FIGURE 3.8 Contrasting methods of solving problems with arithmetic and algebra.

3.6.3 Algebra and Creativity

A principle of this chapter is that teaching needs to proceed from where students are. The section above stressed the transitions that need to be made when students learn to solve problems using algebra and the difficulties that can arise from them. However, it also demonstrated that students can already solve many of the problems which they will later solve by algebra, with creative logical arithmetic reasoning. It is therefore of interest to ask whether students' creativity reduces when they learn routine equation solving methods. Tabach and Friedlander (2013) studied this, by tracking how the creativity of students varied with age. They gave students three problems which can be solved by algebra or otherwise and examined the number of solutions and their variety.

One problem they used was the famous farmyard problem. They asked students to discover different ways to find the number of chickens and cows on a farm if altogether there were 70 heads and 186 feet. Before they learned algebra, students mostly used guess–check–improve methods or used patterns in various, often creative, ways. Compared to younger students, Grade 8 students (in the early stages of learning algebra) used fewer methods, demonstrating mainly algebraic equation solving attempts. However, older students with stronger algebra used the greatest number of methods, returning to the pre-algebra solutions and adding multiple equation solving and graphical solutions. Tabach and Friedlander (2013) summarize their findings by noting that "the learning of algebra might have a temporary limiting effect on creativity, but in the long run, it has the potential to enrich the students' repertoire of solution methods" (p. 238). Teachers who encourage multiple solution methods can help students to gain power and generality but not lose on thought. The problem Arithmogons in Figure 3.14 provides many opportunities for encouraging such creativity.

3.7 The Procedures of Equation Solving

> Dear Algebra, Please stop asking us to find your x. She's never coming back and don't ask y.
>
> (seen on a T-shirt)

A great deal can be said about students learning to solve equations and the difficulties that they have with syntax and applying rules, the common errors and the most successful methods for teaching. Some of these issues are discussed in Chapter 4. However, with the theme of looking at algebra through the eyes of the learner, this section only discusses the underlying ideas.

There are many useful ways of solving equations. The simplest strategy is guess–check–improve, where numbers are input into the equation to check if they provide a solution. Ideally, until a solution is found, careful consideration of the input and output will lead to an improved next guess. Because not all equations can be solved analytically and because digital technology makes calculation for many trials very fast, guess–check–improve is now an important strategy. The Egyptian method shown in Chapter 2 for solving Problem #24 from the Rhind Papyrus is a sophisticated form of guess–check–improve, where the improve step harnesses proportional reasoning. Graphical solutions can be thought of as using a highly organized form of guess-check-improve. Now, as shown in Subsection 5.3.2, digital technology has made graphical solution (where literally thousands of values are calculated and simultaneously displayed) both practical and powerful.

Conceptually, the next simplest method of solving equations is "undoing" the operations which have transformed an unknown number to the given output. For example, the expression $3(x + 4) + 2$ can be understood as instructions for a process: we start with a number (called x), add 4, multiply the result by 3 and add 2. This is shown in the first two rows of Figure 3.9. To solve the equation $3(x + 4) + 2 = 29$, it is simple to work backwards undoing the operations (e.g. by subtracting 2 instead of adding 2), as shown in the third row of the figure, to find that the original value of x was 5. The notion of undoing operations in the opposite order is familiar to young students: in the morning I put on my socks and then my shoes, and at night I take off my shoes and then my socks. The process is also conceptually simple because it is carried out entirely on and with numbers (start with 29, subtract 2, divide by 3, subtract 4). The main difficulty is decoding the algebraic expressions to see what operations have been performed on the unknown number and in what order.

At this early stage, doing the same operation to each side is a way of keeping track of the state of the algebraic expression and the numbers, without drawing the flowchart. However, the thinking is concerned with undoing the operations that were done to the starting number.

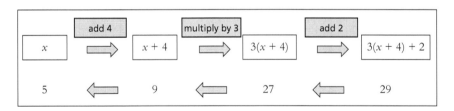

FIGURE 3.9 A flowchart showing "what happened to a number" and how to undo it.

Using algebraic notation, this method would often be shown as follows:

$3(x + 4) + 2 = 29$
$3(x + 4) = 27$ Undoing "add 2" by subtracting 2
$x + 4 = 9$ Undoing "multiply by 3" by dividing by 3
$x = 5$ Undoing "add 4" by subtracting 4 from each side

66 Seeing Algebra Through the Eyes of a Learner

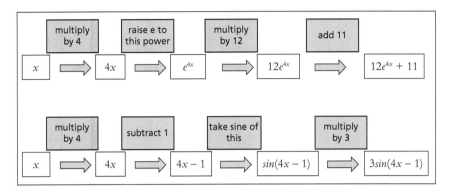

FIGURE 3.10 Flowcharts for complex equations that can be solved by undoing operations.

Undoing operations is a powerful solving technique, which can be applied to simple equations as above or to much more complicated equations. Figure 3.10 shows two examples. Solving equations such as $12e^{4x} + 11 = 13$ and $3\sin(4x - 1) = -2$ only requires the new knowledge of the inverse functions for raising to the power (log) and for sine, but it is otherwise a familiar process.

Although the ideas above can be applied to some complex equations, there are some simple equations where they cannot readily be applied. For example, the method does not work for the equation $3(x + 4) + 2 = 5x$ (see also Subsection 5.3.2). The operations cannot be undone because there is no number to start the undoing operations with, and so equations like this present a "cognitive gap" for students to cross (Linchevski & Herscovics, 1996). The idea that the complex calculations on the left-hand side of the equation produce the result of the right-hand side has to give way to the more sophisticated understanding of equality as a relation, as discussed in Section 3.4.

To solve this equation, we "do the same to both sides" supplemented by appropriate algebraic simplification steps. One such path is shown below.

$3(x + 4) + 2 = 5x$
$3x + 14 = 5x$ simplifying (expanding and collecting like terms)
$14 = 2x$ maintaining equality by subtracting $3x$ from each side
$7 = x$ maintaining equality by taking a half of the quantity on each side
$x = 7$

In addition to involving more algebraic work, in this solution there are important changes of perspective. Instead of working on and with numbers, it is necessary to operate on and with unknowns and expressions (Kieran, 1992). Moreover, the strategy has changed. Instead of undoing operations, the strategy is now to maintain the equality through a series of steps which eventually lead to an equation (in this case $x = 7$) that explicitly shows the value of the unknown. Working with the equality can be well illustrated (in simple cases where the solution is a positive number) by the "balance model" as shown for the above solution in Figure 3.11. Adding or removing equal amounts or equal proportions from each balance pan maintains the balance.

Analyzing the principles behind this solution method returns us to the process–object distinction made earlier in this chapter. For this solution method to make sense to a student, the statement of equality (i.e. the equation) has to become itself a psychological "object" on which operations can be performed. The equation cannot be seen as a process where calculating one side produces the other. Whereas in the first "undoing operations" examples, the operations of undoing were carried out on numbers (maybe keeping track of progress with algebraic expressions), now the operations ("doing the same to both sides") are carried out on whole equations to preserve the equality. This is a psychological leap for students.

Looked at from this point of view, by using the "do the same to both sides" principle of maintaining balance (equality), the series of steps above transforms the equation $3(x + 4) + 2 = 5x$ through a series of equations until a very simple equation (in this case $x = 7$) is reached. The logic is that any value of x which makes the first equation true will make all of the subsequent equations true. Any solution of the first equation will be a solution of the last. Hence the only possible solution of the first equation is 7 (and indeed $3(7 + 4) + 2 = 5 \times 7$).

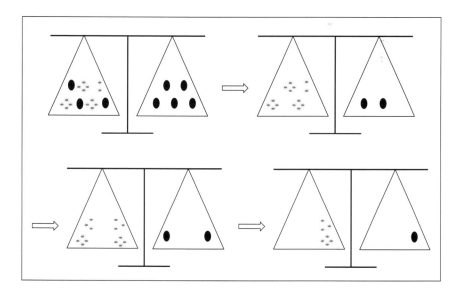

FIGURE 3.11 Solving $3(x + 4) + 2 = 5x$ with a balance model (blobs represent x).

3.7.1 Process–Object Distinction in Solving Simultaneous Equations

This changing focus of what is the object that is being operated upon (letter, expression or equation) becomes clearer and more important beyond solving simple equations. For example, as demonstrated in Section 3.6, the sweets problem can be solved with two simultaneous equations:

Equation 1: $7y - 168 = x$
Equation 2: $4y = x - 36$

The conceptually simplest way to solve these equations is by substitution: replacing x in Equation 2 by $(7y - 168)$ from Equation 1, then finding y from the new equation $4y = (7y - 168) - 36$. In this action, the variable x is replaced by the expression $7y - 168$. As discussed above, students need to see $7y - 168$ as a mathematical object (rather than a process) to do this. And by the time they reach simultaneous equations, most of them do. However, new process–object complexities arise in solving equations by the elimination method, which is why most students find the substitution method easier to understand.

To solve these equations by elimination, we could subtract Equation 2 from Equation 1 to give Equation 3 (in Figure 3.12), then solve Equation 3 to give Equation 4 and the solution (Method 1). Alternatively, we could multiply Equation 1 by 4 and Equation 3 by 7, and then subtract (Method 2). Of course this is less efficient, but it demonstrates that in the elimination method, the objects being operated upon are the equations, not the variables or the expressions. For students to feel confident in the elimination method, they have to successfully negotiate this new level in the ongoing journey which turns mathematical processes into new objects, and then learn how to operate on these new objects. Note that the elimination method is justified because it can be seen as another instance of "do the same to both sides." For example, in Figure 3.12, Equation 3 can be obtained by subtracting $4y$ from both sides: directly on the left-hand side but using the equal amount $x - 36$ on the right-hand side.

Method 1: Eliminating x

Eqn 1:	$7y - 168$	$= x$	→	Eqn 1:	$7y - 168$	$= x$	→	Eqn 4:	$3y$	$= 204$
Eqn 2:	$4y$	$= x - 36$		Eqn 3:	$3y - 168$	$= 36$		Eqn 5:	y	$= 68$
									x	$= 308$

Method 2: Eliminating y

Eqn 1:	$7y - 168$	$= x$	→	Eqn 6:	$28y - 672$	$= 4x$	→	Eqn 8:	924	$= 3x$
Eqn 2:	$4y$	$= x - 36$		Eqn 7:	$28y + 252$	$= 7x$		Eqn 9:	x	$= 308$
									y	$= 68$

FIGURE 3.12 Alternative methods of solving a pair of simultaneous equations.

This section has highlighted some of the ideas that need to be in place for solving problems using equations with understanding. Equation solving demonstrates how students need to be able to unpack algebraic expressions to see the operations which they signify and the order in which they are carried out: a process conception of expressions. They also need to be able to see an expression as an object on which other operations can be performed, and also see an equation as an object on which other operations (operations which preserve the solution set) can be performed. The final example of this process–object transition is taken up in the next section.

3.8 Functions as Processes and Objects

This section examines another of the major concepts of school algebra—that of function. This is the third case in this chapter of the progression from process to object, and so before looking specifically at functions, the general theory is briefly outlined.

All of the elements of mathematics are abstract—none have a physical existence outside of human minds. Even a square is abstract. Real objects can be shaped like squares, but these shapes can never reach the ideal of the mathematical definition of square. Similarly, there are sets of four real things, but four itself does not have any material existence. Yet to do mathematics successfully, the common experience is that geometrical figures, numbers and concepts of much greater complexity must be mathematical objects—things almost as real as if they have a physical presence. Researchers have therefore studied how these abstractions develop and how mathematical objects come to feel real. Sfard (1991, p. 3) is among those who see this process as critical to success in mathematics:

> Unlike material objects, however, advanced mathematical constructs are totally inaccessible to our senses – they can only be seen with our mind's eyes ... Being capable of somehow "seeing" these invisible objects appears to be an essential component of mathematical ability: lack of this capacity may be one of the major reasons because of which mathematics appears practically impermeable to so many "well-formed minds".

Sfard (1991) proposed that most mathematical entities begin as processes and, through a sequence of stages, gradually take on the object-like character, the final stage being called reification. When they become objects, but not before, mathematical entities can be operated upon to make new processes and eventually new objects and in this way much of the great edifice of mathematics is built. The building happens in the head of each individual as well as communally building the discipline of mathematics. The evidence for this theory lies in the history of how some mathematical ideas have developed and in close analysis of students when learning mathematics. The final stage of reification is usually most difficult to achieve (Sfard & Linchevski, 1994). Reification is not confined only to mathematics, but is a general cognitive process. A common example is called "nominalization" in language where we can say "the boys were fighting" or "the boys had a fight." Through nominalization, the action/process of fighting becomes the event/object of a fight.

There are many variations and refinements of this process–object theory, including Dubinsky's APOS (action–process–object–schema) theory (e.g. Arnon et al., 2014) that has roots in the work of Piaget, and the "procept" formulation of Gray and Tall (1994), Gray, Pinto, Pitta, and Tall (1999) and others. They use the terminology "procept" to stress that process and object/concept are complementary ways of viewing mathematical entities and that versatility in switching between the two views is essential. Although the object conception (usually) comes after the process conception, it is not that one is always preferred to the other: both are necessary. Several other terminologies have been used by researchers for similar theories (e.g. operation(al) or procedur(al) instead of process and product, concept(ual) or structural instead of object). These theories also have commonalities with general theories from developmental psychology such as Bruner's (1964) proposal that instruction should proceed from enactive (action-based) representation of the concept to be learned, through iconic (image-based) to symbolic representation (where the concept is named and symbolized).

In the case of functions, the process view is that a function turns an input into an output. Nearly always in school algebra, the inputs and outputs are both real numbers. A function such as $f(x) = (x^2 + 1)^{-1}$ is first seen this way, in a point by point fashion, so that for any input number an output number can be calculated. Students find values of the function and plot points on graphs. Gradually students build an object conception, so that they can think globally about this and other functions, not just think about the effect on individual numbers. The function itself begins to have properties and can be combined with other functions in multiple ways.

Of course, functions are generally encountered not in the abstract but in modeling the real world, when the input and output strongly express the *varying quantity* facet of variable described in Subsection 1.2.3 and the interest is in the co-variation of independent and dependent variables. To return to the income tax example of Section 3.1, a student with the initial "process" conception of function sees it as a way of finding any person's tax payable knowing their income. This might be by applying a formula, looking up a table, or entering the income into an applet on the government website. It requires a more sophisticated underlying concept of function to think about questions that go beyond these "pointwise" concerns, for example, to consider whether and how the marginal rate varies with income and the consequences of such variation on the tax that has to be paid.

As an object conception of function is being attained, students can learn about the general properties of families of functions, and this gives insight into functional behavior in many real world situations. For example, quadratic functions grow faster than linear and cubic functions grow faster than quadratic functions, so increasing the dimensions of a container makes a proportionally larger change in its area and an even larger change in its volume. A small increase in the dimensions of a box can make a surprising difference to the packed weight. Because of the inverse square law, stepping back from a source of heat or other radiation makes a proportionally larger reduction in heat or radiation received. Reducing the number of pixels of height and width of an image by a certain percentage makes a proportionally much larger change in the storage space required for the image. By supporting understandings such as these, the conception of functions as objects, not just as rules for calculation, provides a gateway to understanding phenomena in the scientific, personal, occupational and social domains.

Within pure mathematics, when an object view of functions has been achieved, functions can themselves be the elements that new processes operate upon and new objects can be created. For example, with the processes of pointwise function addition and scalar multiplication, a set of functions can become the elements of a vector space, another mathematical object. Differentiation and integration are also new processes (operations) that can be carried out on suitable functions and they yield answers which are also functions. Differentiation may appear to students to occur at a point (e.g. finding the slope of the tangent at a point), but it is about the whole function (at least locally), not just its value at the relevant point. Students without this understanding will often enter incorrect commands into a computer algebra system when differentiating at a point, as is illustrated in Figure 3.13 with output from TI-Nspire CAS. On the first line, the function is differentiated, then the substitution made. On the second line, the substitution of $x = 3$ occurs, first creating a constant function $h(x) = \frac{1}{10}$, and the derivative of a constant function is the function always equal to zero.

Sfard (1991) points out that the idea of function arose after a long search for a mathematical model for physical quantities involving variable quantities. The essence of the idea was that the dependent variable changed according to changes in the independent variable. Initially, the mathematical formula specifying how function values are calculated was regarded as an essential part of being a function, as it is for the practical examples discussed above. Gradually, however, the idea of a function was broadened so that the rule for calculation was downplayed, and now the commonly accepted mathematical definition of a function is a set of ordered pairs. Functions need to be well defined (i.e. many-to-one) but this does not have to be by any recognizable formula. This definition puts the emphasis on the static

$\frac{d}{dx}\left((x^2+1)^{-1}\right)\|x=3$	$\frac{-3}{50}$
$\frac{d}{dx}\left((x^2+1)^{-1}\|x=3\right)$	0

FIGURE 3.13 CAS output showing a common student error in differentiation.

"object" (the set of pairs) whilst the "process" (the calculations and the rules governing them) are no longer at the forefront of the definition. It seems therefore that there has been a movement over time from a process view to an object view within formal mathematics.

Moschkovich, Schoenfeld and Arcavi (1993) studied how students develop an understanding of functions and their graphs. They investigated learning the different representations of linear functions (tables, symbols and graphs) and the acquisition of the process perspective (linking individual x and y values, plotting points) and the object perspective (the function concept itself, the symbolic representation and the global properties of the graph). The study used function graphing software, so that students could easily manipulate graphs as objects and develop an intuitive feel for global properties such as slope, without their attention always being drawn to the pointwise calculations. Careful observation of students' problem solutions showed that learning about functions is not just a matter of first learning the process perspective (how to calculate values and plot points) and then acquiring an object perspective that is better. Instead they found that an important part of developing competency requires learning to move flexibly between the process and object perspectives, and being able to select the best perspective to achieve a desired end. This flexibility was slow developing: good students often faltered at the stage of problem solving where a switch between process and object perspectives was called for. Such flexibility is expressed in the "procept" idea of Gray and Tall above. Chapter 5 discusses how new technologies can influence both process and object views of algebraic entities.

Learning about functions involves much more than the transitions between process and object. The notation is complex, there are graphical and tabular representations to coordinate with the symbolic representation, and there are many special types of functions. Individual families of functions deserve special treatment and have special properties to learn about. However, developing the idea that a function is one object, not just a lot of calculations, is an important foundation for future mathematics that takes time to fully develop.

3.9 Chapter Summary

Algebra involves a new way of thinking that requires substantial change of perspective, alongside the considerable manipulative rule-based skills required to deal fluently and accurately with its notation. Students come to algebra after learning arithmetic, which of course provides essential skills for doing algebra. Perhaps surprisingly, however, the transition from arithmetic to algebra is not a smooth one. It is not just that the new algebra ideas are hard; it is also that many of the well-established ideas from arithmetic apply, but only when given an unfamiliar twist. Beginning students also bring to the learning of algebra their ideas about letters in other forms of writing. Algebra is a language particularly suited to explicitly describing mathematical relationships and structure. This too is a new orientation for students, who have previously dealt with structure only intuitively.

As students learn algebra, they need to go through several cycles where mathematical processes are turned into mathematical objects. As they put on the new algebra spectacles, they begin to see algebraic entities that they could not see before. The first is that algebraic expressions need to be seen as objects, rather than as instructions for what to do with a number. Then equations have to change from a shorthand way of writing mathematical facts, to mathematical objects which themselves can be operated upon. Functions similarly are first encountered as rules for transforming numbers, but later become objects in their own right which have properties and can be transformed and combined to form other functions. Many entities in all branches of mathematics are created in this way.

This chapter has reviewed some of the transitions that students need to make to move to the new way of thinking. Knowledge of what students bring to algebra can help teachers address issues that underlie student difficulties. Both students and their teachers have to work hard so that students can learn to see through their new very powerful algebra spectacles.

3.10 Thinking Further

All Sections

1. Present some students with some of the mathematical tasks that have been analyzed in this chapter, asking them to think aloud as they work. Listen carefully and observe their written work with as little intervention as possible. Audio or videoing students as they work might be possible. Do you observe the phenomena reported in this chapter? Can the ideas of this chapter help you to analyze and explain your observations?
2. Examine the research literature about students' thinking for other aspects of algebra, such as common manipulative errors and their causes. The research on learning and teaching algebra is now both wide and deep.
3. Consider the following memories from a learner of algebra: "I remember one day after I had been learning algebra for about 3 years. I noticed that I had started to check some arithmetic calculations with algebra whereas before I always used to check my algebra with arithmetic." What do you think this insight may mean for a student?

Section 3.2 What Do Algebraic Letters Represent?

4. Look for instances of "fruit salad algebra" and other instances of misleading teaching in instructional resources that are used in local schools.

Section 3.3 The Process–Object Duality

5. Present the items in this section to some students beginning algebra. Interview some students who make conjoining errors. Do their explanations of their difficulty support the claims in this section?

Section 3.4 The Meaning of the Equals Sign

6. Look for the ways in which the equals sign is used in instructional resources that are used in local schools for students learning algebra and for younger students. When does the equals sign have to be used with a full sense of equality, rather than as an instruction to find an answer?

Section 3.5 Algebra for Recording and Revealing Mathematical Structure

7. Generalize the problem of Mark and Jan sharing money to three people. Together Mark, Jan and Dan get T, but Mark gets D more than Jan and E more than Dan. Rearrange the algebraic expressions for the solutions to show and justify two methods: one where the first action is to give Mark his extra money and one where the first action is to give each person a third of the money. Explain these procedures. Generalize to more than three people.
8. Investigate Arithmogon puzzles to explore how algebraic expressions reveal and reflect mathematical structure. To make an Arithmogon, draw a large triangle and put a matchbox at each vertex. Inside each box hide some beans, keeping the number secret. A triangle showing one set of numbers of beans (6, 12 and 7) is shown in Figure 3.14. On each side of the triangle write the total number of beans on its two vertices. To make an Arithmogon puzzle, hide the beans in each box, showing just the numbers on the sides and challenge your friend to find the number of beans at each vertex. Figure 3.14 shows the creation of such a puzzle: start with the beans in the boxes at the vertices, calculate the totals, hide the beans and present the puzzle to your friend. The general task is to find a rule to solve any Arithmogon puzzle. (For older students, there is no need to always use positive whole numbers of beans.)

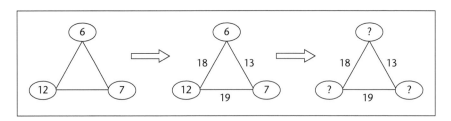

FIGURE 3.14 How to make an Arithmogon puzzle.

(a) Solve the Arithmogon puzzle in Figure 3.14 in as many ways as you can.
(b) Let the secret numbers of beans be a, b and c and let A, B and C be the known numbers on the opposite sides so that $A = b + c$, $B = c + a$ and $C = a + b$. Solve this Arithmogon puzzle using algebra. Remember that A, B and C are knowns and a, b and c are the unknowns that have to be found.
(c) Show, from the equations that $A + B + C = 2(a + b + c)$. Use beans to explain the reason for this relationship.
(d) One way of writing the algebraic solution for a is $a = \frac{1}{2}B + \frac{1}{2}C - \frac{1}{2}A$. Use beans to explain why this is a solution.
(e) Another way of writing the algebraic solution for a is $a = \frac{1}{2}(A + B + C) - A$. Use beans to explain why this is a solution. (Hint: What is $\frac{1}{2}(A + B + C)$ in terms of beans?)
(f) Generalization: Investigate Arithmogons where the starting shape is not a triangle but a square or a pentagon or other polygons.
(g) With colleagues, compare and contrast the features of the many methods of solving Arithmogon puzzles.

Section 3.6 Transitions From Learning Arithmetic to Learning Algebra

9. Select some students in the school year before algebra begins. Watch them solve some word problems in Section 3.6 that can be solved with linear equations, such as the stamps and sweets problems and the farmyard problem. Observe the variety of solutions that they use. You may be able to examine creativity following the methods used by Tabach and Friedlander (2013).
10. The problem below is from the Singapore Primary School Leaving Examination. Note that P5(6) is Grade 5(6) in Singapore. Solve the problem with algebra and then without algebra using the model method. Analyze the difficulties that are encountered in using each method.

    The participants in a competition are P5 and P6 pupils in the ratio of 2:1. All the P5 participants are girls. Among the P6 participants, the ratio of girls to boys is 4:3. There are 30 more P5 girls than P6 girls taking part in the competition. How many participants in the competition are girls?
    (Primary School Leaving Examination item quoted by Dindyal [2006, p. 182])

Section 3.7 The Procedures of Equation Solving

11. Explore what types of equations in one variable can be solved by drawing flowcharts and then "undoing" operations. Do not allow first changing the algebraic form (e.g. do not first change $4x - 2 - x = 1$ into $3x - 2 = 10$ before creating the flowchart). Consider three categories: suitable for this method; awkward with this method; unsuitable for this method.
12. Discuss the relative merits of teaching students to solve equations with the mnemonic "change side, change sign" or the mnemonic "do the same to both

sides." Consider conceptual and procedural issues, including the process–object duality. Illustrate your discussion with well-chosen examples.

13. Solve the problem below by:
    (a) drawing a flowchart as in Figure 3.9, then undoing the operations, then
    (b) setting up a set of simultaneous equations and solving them, then
    (c) setting up an equation in one unknown and solving it.
    Compare and contrast the knowledge and strategies that are required by each of the three methods.
    A woman has a certain number of dollar bills in her purse. She has no other money. She spends half the money on a hat and gives $1 to a beggar outside the store. She spends half the remaining dollars on lunch and tips the waiter $2. She then spends half the remaining dollars on a book, and just before she goes home she spends $3 on a hot fudge sundae. She now has $1 left. How many dollars did she begin with?

14. There are three well-known methods for solving quadratic equations: (1) using the quadratic formula, (2) completing the square and (3) factorizing and then using the null factor law. The first two parts of this task show that using "the formula" is a packaged version of completing the square, and the underlying equation solving principle for both is "undoing operations." Solving by factorizing has a different underlying principle, explored in part (c) below.
    (a) Demonstrate the link between method (1) and method (2) by showing how to derive the quadratic formula by completing the square. The geometrical insights from Al-Khwarizmi in Section 2.4 may assist.
    (b) Show that "completing the square" enables any quadratic equation to be solved by "undoing" operations. (See also Section 4.6.)
    (c) Prove the null factor law, which is the basis of method (3) from the field axioms for real numbers. Hint: The field axioms state that all numbers other than 0 have both an additive inverse and a multiplicative inverse and that $1 \times x = x$ for all x. First prove that $0 \times x = 0$ for all x by considering $x = 1 \times x = (1 + 0) \times x$ and assuming the distributive law as an axiom. Then combine this information with the axiom that all non-zero numbers have a multiplicative inverse to show that if $ab = 0$ then either $a = 0$ or $b = 0$.

15. Sometimes special properties of the solution can be used to solve equations better than simple theory predicts. Diophantine equations (equations where all the solutions must be integers) are like this. For example, the equation $\frac{1}{n} + \frac{1}{m} = \frac{1}{6}$ has two variables, and an infinite number of solutions. However, as a Diophantine equation, there are only five positive integer solutions. Find these solutions. How many solutions are there if negative integers are allowed?
    ○ Hint 1: Transform the equation to $(n - 6)(m - 6) = 36$ and then note that the integers $n - 6$ and $m - 6$ must be factors of 36. OR

- Hint 2: Express n as a function of m, as follows $n = \frac{6m}{m-6}$ then consider the shape of the resulting hyperbola, and check the finite number of possible points with integer coefficients that could lie on it.

Section 3.8 Functions as Processes and Objects

16. In some countries, students begin algebra by learning about equation solving, so that the first idea of a letter is the idea of an unknown number. In other countries students begin algebra by learning about functions, so that the first idea of a letter is as a variable. Discuss the relative advantages and disadvantages of each of these approaches.

3.11 References

Arcavi, A. (1994). Symbol sense: Informal sense-making in formal mathematics. *For the Learning of Mathematics, 14*(3), 24–35.

Arcavi, A. (2005). Developing and using symbol sense in mathematics. *For The Learning of Mathematics, 25*(2), 42–47.

Arnon, I., Cottrill, J., Dubinsky, E., Oktaç, A., Roa Fuentes, S., Trigueros, M., & Weller, K. (2014). *APOS Theory: A Framework for Research and Curriculum Development in Mathematics Education.* Dordrecht: Springer.

Behr, M., Erlwanger, S., & Nichols, E. (1980). How children view the equal sign. *Mathematics Teaching, 92*, 13–15.

Boyer, C. B. (1968). *A History of Mathematics.* New York: Wiley.

Bruner, J. S. (1964). The course of cognitive growth. *American Psychologist, 19*(1), 1–15.

Cai, J., & Knuth, E. (Eds.) (2011). *Early Algebraization.* Berlin: Springer-Verlag.

Carpenter, T., Franke, M., & Levi, L. (2003). *Thinking Mathematically: Integrating Arithmetic & Algebra in Elementary School.* Portsmount, NH: Heinemann.

Collis, K. F. (1974). *Cognitive Development and Mathematics Learning.* Paper presented at the Psychology of Mathematics Workshop, Center for Science Education, Chelsea College, London.

Descartes, R. (1925). *La Géometrie.* Translated by David E. Smith and Marcia L. Latham. Chicago: Open Court Publishing.

Dindyal, J. (2006). The Singaporean Mathematics Curriculum: Connections to TIMSS. In P. Grootenboer, R. Zevenbergen & M. Chinnappan (Eds.), *Proceedings of the 29th Annual Conference of the Mathematics Education Research Group of Australasia* (pp. 179–186). Canberra: MERGA. www.merga.net.au/documents/RP182006.pdf (accessed August 31, 2015).

Foy, P., Arora, A., & Stanco, G. (Eds.) (2013). *TIMSS 2011 User Guide for the International Database. Released Items. Mathematics – Eighth Grade.* Boston: TIMSS & PIRLS International Study Center.

Gould, S. J. (1991). *Bully for Brontosaurus.* New York: W.W. Norton.

Gray, E., & Tall, D. (1994). Duality, ambiguity, and flexibility: A "proceptual" view of simple arithmetic. *Journal for Research in Mathematics Education, 25*(2), 116–140.

Gray, E., Pinto, M., Pitta, D., & Tall, D. (1999). Knowledge construction and diverging thinking in elementary & advanced mathematics. *Educational Studies in Mathematics, 38*(1), 111–133.

Hodgen, J., Küchemann, D., Brown, M., & Robert Coe, R. (2008). Children's understandings of algebra 30 years. In M. Joubert (Ed.), *Proceedings of the British Society for Research into Learning Mathematics*. Retrieved from www.bsrlm.org.uk/IPs/ip28-3/BSRLM-IP-28-3-07.pdf (accessed August 31, 2015).

Kaput, J. J., Carraher, D. W., & Blanton, M. L. (Eds.) (2008). *Algebra in the Early Grades*. New York: Lawrence Erlbaum.

Kiasu Parents (n.d.). *2012 PSLE Discussions and Strategy*. Retrieved from www.kiasuparents.com/kiasu/phpbb3/viewtopic.php?f=69&t=24263&hilit=burn&start=210 (accessed August 31, 2015).

Kieran, C. (1981). Concepts associated with the equality symbol. *Educational Studies in Mathematics, 12*(3), 317–326.

Kieran, C. (1992). The learning and teaching of school algebra. In D. A. Grouws (Ed.), *Handbook of Research on Mathematics Teaching and Learning* (pp. 390–419). New York: Macmillan.

Kierkegaard, S. (1859/1998). *The Point of View: Kierkegaard's Writings, Vol. 22*. Princeton: Princeton University Press.

Knuth, E. J., Stephens, A., McNeil, N., & Alibali, M. (2006). Does understanding the equal sign matter? Evidence from solving equations. *Journal for Research in Mathematics Education, 37*(4), 297–312.

Küchemann, D. (1981). Algebra. In K. M. Hart (Ed.), *Children's Understanding of Mathematics, 11–16* (pp. 102–119). Oxford, London: Alden Press.

Linchevski, L., & Herscovics, N. (1996). Crossing the cognitive gap between arithmetic and algebra: Operating on the unknown in the context of equations. *Educational Studies in Mathematics, 30*(1), 39–65.

MacGregor, M. (1986). A fresh look at fruit salad. *The Australian Mathematics Teacher, 42*(3), 9–11.

MacGregor, M., & Stacey, K. (1997). Students' understanding of algebraic notation: 11–16. *Educational Studies in Mathematics, 33*(1), 1–19.

Moschkovich, J., Schoenfeld, A., & Arcavi, A. (1993). Aspects of understanding: On multiple perspectives and representations of linear relations and connections among them. In T. A. Romberg, E. Fennema & T. P. Carpenter (Eds.), *Integrating Research on the Graphical Representation of Functions* (pp. 69–100). Hillsdale, NJ: Lawrence Erlbaum.

Ray, J. (1886). *New Elementary Algebra. Primary Elements of Algebra for Common Schools and Academies*. New York: American Book Company. Retrieved from http://books.google.co.il/books?id=Go8AAAAAMAAJ&pg=PR1&hl=iw&source=gbs_selected_pages&cad=2#v=onepage&q&f=false (accessed August 31, 2015).

Sfard, A. (1991). On the dual nature of mathematical conceptions: Reflections on processes and objects as different sides of the same coin. *Educational Studies in Mathematics, 22*(1), 1–36.

Sfard, A., & Linchevski, L. (1994). The gains and the pitfalls of reification: The case of algebra. *Educational Studies in Mathematics, 26*(2), 191–228.

Stacey, K., & MacGregor, M. (2000). Learning the algebraic method of solving problems. *Journal of Mathematical Behavior*, 18(2), 149–167.

Stacey, K., Chick, H., & Kendal, M. (Eds.), (2004). *The Future of the Teaching and Learning of Algebra: The 12th ICMI Study*. Dordrecht: Kluwer.

Stacey, K., Steinle, V., Price, B., & Gvozdenko, E. (n.d.). *Specific Mathematics Assessments that Reveal Thinking*. Retrieved from www.smartvic.com (accessed August 31, 2015).

Steinle, V., Gvozdenko, E., Price, B., Stacey, K., & Pierce, R. (2009). Investigating students' numerical misconceptions in algebra. In R. Hunter, B. Bicknell, & T. Burgess (Eds.),

Crossing Divides: Proceedings of the 32nd Annual Conference of the Mathematics Education Research Group of Australasia, Vol. 2. Palmerston North, NZ: MERGA.

Tabach, M., & Friedlander, A. (2013). School mathematics and creativity at the elementary and middle-grade levels: How are they related? *ZDM, 45*, 227–238.

The Math Forum. (n.d.) *Ask Dr. Math*. Retrieved from http://mathforum.org/library/drmath/view/56834.html (accessed August 31, 2015).

Watanabe, T. (2011). Shiki: A critical foundation for school algebra in Japanese elementary school mathematics. In J. Cai & E. Knuth (Eds.), *Early Algebraization* (pp. 109–124). Berlin: Springer.

Yeap, B.-H. (2010). *A glimpse into mathematics Teaching & Learning in Singapore Elementary Schools*. Retrieved from http://math.nie.edu.sg/t3/downloads/A_Glimpse_Into_Singapore_Math.pdf (accessed September 3, 2014).

4

EMPHASES IN ALGEBRA TEACHING

> There is a stage in the curriculum when the introduction of algebra may make simple things hard, but not teaching algebra will soon render it impossible to make hard things simple.
>
> (Tall & Thomas, 1991, p. 128)

4.1 Introduction

In the previous chapters, algebraic activity is characterized by actions of representing and manipulating. In these actions, the core algebraic objects in play are variable, expression, equation, function and graph. In Chapter 3, some of these key concepts, each with its own issues in the eyes of learners, have been addressed. The present chapter takes a more global stance with respect to the challenge of teaching algebra. It focuses on overarching questions that teachers are faced with throughout the algebra curriculum, including: how to teach algebra in context, how to practice, how to reconcile procedural fluency and algebraic insight, how to tackle well-known student difficulties, and how to deal with proofs in algebra. It is these questions and dilemmas encountered while teaching algebra that will be addressed in this chapter's subsequent sections, illustrated by examples.

These overarching questions and dilemmas are part of what is called pedagogical content knowledge. Shulman (1987) described many categories of knowledge that teachers need, including subject matter content knowledge (CK), general pedagogical knowledge (PK) and a third category, pedagogical content knowledge (PCK). The latter is a special blend of subject matter knowledge combined with directly relevant knowledge of students and their cognitive development and of potential resources for teaching. For teachers of mathematics, their subject matter knowledge will be shared with many other experts (mathematicians, engineers, accountants), their pedagogical knowledge will be shared with teachers of all other subjects, but their pedagogical content knowledge is unique to them as mathematics teachers. This chapter therefore aims to build understanding of difficulties of algebra education and a repertoire of ways to deal with them—an important part of pedagogical content knowledge for teaching algebra.

Does having pedagogical content knowledge assist with good teaching and hence with improved outcomes for students? Many studies confirm this, including a large study by Baumert et al. (2010) which followed 181 teachers of Grade 10 mathematics in Germany for a year. The study found that teachers' PCK had the greatest effect on student achievement and that CK was important especially because poor CK limits the development of PCK. Teachers with good PCK scored highly on the two key variables of instructional quality—the level of cognitive challenge and individual learning support. Teachers with good PCK can understand students' thinking so that they can plan instruction to bring students to the next level in their learning, and they can quickly identify the causes of students' errors and design teaching to address the root cause.

4.2 Teaching Algebra in Context

It is a widely accepted assumption that the learning of algebra can benefit from the students' perception of a sense of purpose. Because of its abstract character, algebra is not an easy subject to teach as such, particularly when algebra is often presented without any context, but as "naked" equations and formula. One way to provide for students' perceiving the purpose of algebra is to have them work on tasks that have "a meaningful outcome for the learners themselves and provide them with the feeling of empowerment that enables them to understand situations which otherwise will remain partially understood or totally opaque" (see Section 1.3). In an attempt to do so, algebra, particularly for younger students, is often presented in contexts. Meaningful problem situations that involve some modeling and in which algebra can be applied form the starting point of algebraic activity. In this section, we deal with two dilemmas that teachers may find themselves confronted with while teaching algebra in context:

- How to deal with the problem's authenticity to convey a sense of purpose?
- How do abstract problem situations as an entrance to algebra fit in?

To start to discuss the first issue, we consider three examples, the first of which is shown in Figure 4.1. At a first glance, this task seems to be linked to a real life context. In reality, however, adding strips of grass to one's lawn starts with a plan, and with an idea of its width, whereas the task's phrasing suggests that the work started without any plan. In particular, it seems unrealistic to set the targeted area to 204 m^2 and to measure the dimensions of the lawn after its extension to verify this: why not immediately measure the width of the strips we want to know? That would avoid the need to multiply the extended dimensions 12 and 17, and, moreover, to solve the quadratic equation and to enter the domain of algebra! In

82 Emphases in Algebra Teaching

> The lawn in a garden measures 10 by 15 meters. The owner decides to extend the lawn. To two sides he adds a strip of equal width of x meters. See the figure below.
>
> a. Show that the area of the enlarged lawn can be represented by
>   Area = $x^2 + 25x + 150$.
> b. The new lawn has an area of 204 m². Set up an equation and calculate the width of the strip.

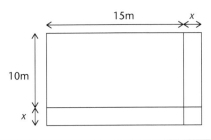

FIGURE 4.1 A non-authentic context: the "extending the lawn" task.

this sense, the problem situation is not authentic, but appears a rather artificial way to invite students to solving an algebraic equation. As such, this is not a helpful pedagogical approach for engaging students into applying algebra to reality, or for fostering students' seeing the purpose of algebra.

One may wonder if students suffer from the lack of reality in this task, and in many other tasks found in current textbooks. The task provides a context that may serve as an entrance into equation solving. However, the danger is that students just get used to reading through problem situations, extracting the algebraic task intended by the textbook author, and solving it, which seems to be part of the "didactical contract" in algebra teaching. However, what students take from such activities is that doing algebra comes down to finding your way through unrealistic stories while trying to fulfill the author's intentions, instead of using algebra as an empowering tool for solving authentic problems. The latter rather than the former should be the ambition of mathematics education.

As a second and less artificial example, we consider the problem of constructing metal beams for a roof structure, which for reasons of strength consist of rods welded into a triangular pattern (Wijers et al., 2006; Drijvers, Dekker, & Wijers, 2011). The task consists of expressing the relationship between the number of rods and the length of the beam in an equation. Even if this task is clearly not a real construction task, the situation was perceived meaningful and authentic by students, also because illustrations of real roof constructions were added. Figure 4.2 shows some different algebraic formulas the students constructed, each reflecting different solution strategies. In these equations, N stands for the number of rods needed for a beam of length L, and the length L corresponds to the total number of triangular bases that are used to form the beam. The first equation, set up by students, expresses the construction of the beam from L triangles (hence $3L$ sides) by a row

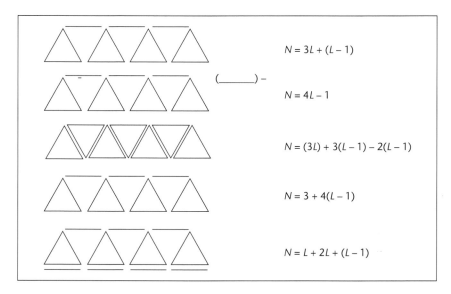

FIGURE 4.2 Building beams with triangles of rods (adapted from Drijvers, Dekker, & Wijers, 2011).

of $L - 1$ connectors across the top. The second equation reflects the strategy of adding one rod to build L "units" of four rods each, and finally subtracting the rod initially added. For teaching purposes, such a diversity of solutions forms an excellent basis for a rich classroom discussion: which of the solutions are correct? How can each of the students explain his or her approach? Which one is the easiest? How can one equation be derived from another? In short, this provides excellent opportunities to informally discuss the notion of equivalence and to practice rewriting expressions.

If we consider school as part of students' and teachers' real lives, the following third example is quite realistic. A class of thirty students did a test for which a maximum score of 80 points could be obtained. The teacher corrected the test papers and entered the score points in her class spreadsheet. However, the scores should be transformed into grades, ranging from 1 to 10. A score of 0 should result in a grade of 1, a score of 80 points in a grade of 10 and the transformation is supposed to be linear. Which formula should the teacher enter in her spreadsheet to have this transformation carried out automatically for the whole class? Clearly, an algebraic formula such as $grade = 1 + 9 \times \frac{score}{80}$ is very helpful here and shows the expressive power of algebra. Other well-known real life applications of elementary algebraic formulas include situations on expressions for prices including and excluding a tax, or on the interplay between fixed and variable costs, for instance to calculate break-even points. In addition to this, algebra, of course, also plays an important role in scientific contexts. To find problem situations in which algebra is really helpful in organizing and solving them is a matter of what Freudenthal (1983) calls didactical phenomenology. It is a challenge for teachers and textbook authors.

The three examples above show that finding and using authentic and realistic contexts is a subtle matter. What some students may perceive as realistic may seem unrealistic to others, depending on their previous experiences and preliminary knowledge of the context and of algebra. Students' experiences may be different and much will depend on the presentation, the phrasing and the timing of the problem. In line with Van den Heuvel-Panhuizen and Drijvers (2013), we make a plea for using the word "realistic" in the sense of "imaginable for students" rather than "referring to real life." Concerning authenticity, an important criterion is that students perceive the task as purposeful and meaningful, and experience that algebra empowers them to solve it. Tasks that are purposeful can be characterized as having "a meaningful outcome for the learner, in terms of an actual or virtual product, the solution of an engaging problem, or an argument or justification for a point of view" (Ainley, Bills, & Wilson, 2005, p. 194). To deal with the task's authenticity, it seems important that the problem situations make sense to the students, that the questions are not artificial and that the use of algebra really contributes to answering these questions.

As students get older and become more advanced in mathematics, problem situations not always need to be related to realistic and authentic contexts, but may have a more abstract character. We address three examples, two from the world of numbers and one from geometry.

The first of these abstract examples is rooted in arithmetic. Students are asked to calculate $2 \times 2 - 1 \times 3$, $3 \times 3 - 2 \times 4$, $4 \times 4 - 5 \times 3$, and so on, and will notice that the result always equals 1. Why would this be the case? This may invite phrasing the property in a general form: $a^2 - (a + 1) \times (a - 1) = 1$. Of course, this identity needs a proof which is easily obtained by expanding and simplifying the expression on the left-hand side. In the task shown in Figure 4.3 this property can be used for estimation. It also concerns the area of a rectangular field, as was the case for the one in Figure 4.1, but this just helps the students to visualize the situation, and is not referring to reality. Hopefully, the students will notice that $31 \times 29 = 30^2 - 1$. Of course, this task can be repeated for other dimensions, such as 51×49, and 101×99. Students may be surprised by the constant absolute error, which is 1 in each of these cases (the relative error is not constant, but that's another story). Further extensions can be found by estimating the outcomes of 52×48 and 102×98. The meaning and the power of algebra here, is that it enables us to prove this phenomenon of arithmetic regularity in a general way, without the need to check all cases one by one. This is quite an intellectual achievement, which also contributes to perceiving algebra as purposeful.

A rectangular field has a length of 31 m and a width of 29 m.
Give a fast estimation (in m^2) of the area.
How many m^2 does this estimation deviate from the exact area?

FIGURE 4.3 Another task on a field (Kindt, 2004).

Speaking about intellectual achievement, a well-known category of algebra problems concerns the so-called THOANs: Think Of A Number problems. As a second example from the world of numbers, think of a number, add 1, double the result, add 3, subtract 4, add 5, halve the result, subtract 2 and subtract the number you first thought of (adapted from Mason, 2005). No matter the starting number, the result will always be 1. Algebra offers the tools to prove this. Similar tasks may concern age problems: my father is twice as old as I am myself, and together we are 75. How old am I? The latter category of problems may invite some numerical trial-and-improve strategies, and as a consequence may be less suitable for demonstrating the meaning and the power of algebra. THOANs and similar problems have the advantage of being both puzzling and challenging to students, and of linking algebra to arithmetic. These tasks can be intriguing to students, as the aim is to uncover the "trick" behind a surprising "magic" phenomenon, even if they are not meaningful in the real life sense.

The third example of abstract problem situations in which algebra can be used concerns a geometrical situation. Figure 4.4 shows an example, adapted from Drijvers, Goddijn, and Kindt (2011). Key to solving this task is the idea that the slope of the line is $\frac{a^2-b^2}{a-b}$, which equals $a + b$. The latter step calls on the rule for the difference of squares, a basic algebraic formula that students should recognize. As the slope of the line remains unchanged, $a + b$ is constant, and, as a consequence, $\frac{a+b}{2}$ is constant as well. But this is the x-coordinate of the midpoint. Therefore, we conclude that the midpoint indeed remains on the vertical line whose equation is $x = \frac{a+b}{2}$. Clearly, this is an abstract problem situation from geometry and not part of real life. Whether this is an obstacle to perceiving algebra as purposeful and meaningful depends on the target group. We expect that the students whom we present this task to have already encountered many parabolas in their mathematics lessons, so that parabolas form a meaningful point of departure for a mathematical task. Parabolas are, so to say, "real in these students' minds." Particularly for more advanced students, intra-mathematical problem situations that make sense to them and connect to previous knowledge may be suitable to show how algebra really "does the job." The algebraic solution to this task is more concise and simple than the geometrical solution (for a geometrical solution see Lockwood, 1961).

To summarize this section, we believe it is important in algebra teaching to emphasize its purpose and meaning to students. Authentic contexts, for example, taken from real life, can invite such algebraic activity. Artificial contexts should be avoided, or at least acknowledged as such, and authenticity may be subject to students' experience and preliminary knowledge. As a consequence, the presentation, phrasing and timing of context problems are crucial. At a more advanced level, or for the sake of intellectual achievement, abstract problem situations (e.g., from the world of numbers or from geometry) may serve as appropriate entrances to or applications of algebra as well.

> A parabola with the equation $y = x^2$ is intersected by a straight line. Using software for dynamic geometry, we move the line upwards, while its slope remains unchanged. The midpoint of the intersection points seems to move on a vertical line. Can we be sure that this is really the case?

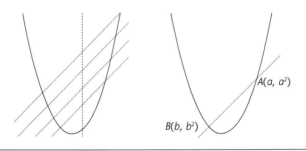

FIGURE 4.4 The cutting a parabola task (adapted from Drijvers, Goddijn, & Kindt, 2011).

As a teacher, one can deal with algebra in context in several ways. First, while preparing a lesson, the teacher can critically consider applications of algebra in tasks and textbooks, and try to avoid artificial or "pseudo-real life" problem situations that will not make students experience algebra as meaningful. Second, a challenge for the teacher is to identify authentic, appropriate and suitable problem situations that do show the purpose of algebra. Naturally, what is suitable depends on the age, level and interests of the target group. Inspiration for problem situations can be found in available (online) resources, but may also emerge from dialogues with colleague teachers in, for example, science and other related subjects. Often, realistic problem situations require a process of transformation or translation from the context world into the world of mathematics and, after the problem solving process, vice versa. This is called formulation and interpretation in the modeling cycle (Niss, Blum, & Galbraith, 2007), or horizontal mathematization in the theory of Realistic Mathematics Education (Freudenthal, 1991; Treffers, 1987). It clearly requires attention and guidance by the teacher. Third, games and puzzles can be authentic environments for algebra because they evoke students' imagination and interest. Just don't present them as realistic. Fourth and final, algebra education includes more than applying algebra. Teaching algebra also means helping students to develop an abstract mental world of algebraic objects and relationships. This process of building up abstract algebra is embedded in the problem solving phase of the modeling cycle, and can be considered as vertical mathematization (Freudenthal, 1991; Treffers, 1987). The level and speed of this process also depend on the target group, but in any case require specific attention by the teacher.

4.3 Productive Practice

It is widely accepted that the mastery of algebra requires practice. But what kind of practice? Should it focus on the acquisition of automated procedural skills, or on flexible algebraic thinking? It is not self-evident that the two go hand in hand: tasks that focus on procedural skills in a routine-like way usually do not appeal to insightful application. There can even be a tension between automatization and insight, which Freudenthal phrases as follows:

> I have observed, not only with other people but also with myself ... that sources of insight can be clogged by automatism. One finally masters an activity so perfectly that the question of how and why is not asked any more, cannot be asked any more, and is not even understood any more as a meaningful and relevant question.
>
> *(Freudenthal, 1983, p. 469)*

On the one hand, we want students to be able to carry out basic procedures "without thinking"; on the other hand, we expect them to remain alert and to notice eventual deviations from the standardized pathways. Li (1999) paraphrases the well-known English proverb "practice makes perfect" while wondering: does practice make perfect, stupid or boring? While answering this question, he is quite clear that he is not against practicing procedural skills: "Manipulative practice is the genetic place of mathematical thinking and the foundation of concept formation" (Li, 1999, p. 35).

In search for practice that helps to make perfect but does not make the students follow the rules inappropriately or just bores them, we need tasks that do address practicing skills, but in the meantime encourage students' alertness, creativity or thinking. In line with this, Friedlander and Arcavi (2012, p. 609) suggest adding "a conceptual dimension to the practice of algebraic procedures." They propose practice-oriented activities that "require the adoption of some additional higher-order thinking skills, such as developing alternative solutions, evaluating the effectiveness of approaches, participating in class discussions, and reflecting on learned procedures and solution methods" (Friedlander & Arcavi, 2012, p. 609). In this section, we address tasks that involve both sides of this coin of algebraic proficiency.

As a means to achieve this integrated practice of procedural fluency and algebraic insight, Kindt (2004, 2011) proposes what he calls productive practice tasks. Where practice in many cases may have a reproductive character in that students repeat procedures shown in worked examples, productive practice comes down to providing students with more challenging tasks in which these procedures are used to produce something, to create. Productive practice tasks provide students with the opportunity to integrate procedural skills with their insightful, flexible and creative application. Let us consider some exemplary tasks that offer productive practice.

As a first example, we could imagine the task in Figure 4.5 to be worked on after students practiced expanding brackets in the products of two linear expressions.

> In the following four lines, place parentheses, if needed, to the left of the equals sign to create an equality.
>
> $a + 2 \cdot a + 7 = 3a + 7$
> $a + 2 \cdot a + 7 = 3a + 14$
> $a + 2 \cdot a + 7 = a^2 + 2a + 7$
> $a + 2 \cdot a + 7 = a^2 + 9a + 14$

FIGURE 4.5 Task to position parentheses (Kindt, 2011).

In this case, the reverse question is: how to place parentheses to create equality? This reverse task requires some flexible thinking, whereas the students in the meantime practice the procedural skill of expanding brackets. It shares important characteristics with the task of completing missing spaces designed by Friedlander and Arcavi (2012) and described in Figure 1.13. As does Kindt, these authors also make a plea for reverse thinking as a means to focus students on the meaning of what they are doing, rather than on automatization.

As a second example, the task shown in Figure 4.6 might fit in a teaching sequence on algebraic fractions. First, when two algebraic fractions are simplified, the results are the same (although the domains are different). This raises a less routine and more productive question: find other algebraic fractions that can be simplified to the same expression. This might be an unexpected "complexification" task for students, and contributes to some variation in the practice. An important aspect of such a task is that there are many correct answers. In a class, the variety of responses may be an excellent entrance to a whole-class discussion on the correctness of the different answers, their compatibility and the ways students found them. Such whole-class discussions are an important means to synthesize learning and provide the teacher with opportunities to capitalize on the results of the practice activity.

The third example is also based on Kindt (2011). Students are asked to square the expression $x + 6$, which leads to $x^2 + 12x + 36$. Next, the task is to subtract 1 and to factor the result. This leads to the final answer of $(x + 5)(x + 7)$. So far, so good, procedural skill, definitely. Next, however, students are asked to repeat this chain of operations for expressions such as $x + 4$, $y + 10$ and $z + 11$. This is expected to reveal a somewhat surprising phenomenon. Students are asked to find

> The algebraic fractions $\dfrac{1}{1+\dfrac{1}{x}}$ and $\dfrac{x^2+x}{x^2+2x+1}$ can both be reduced to $\dfrac{x}{x+1}$.
>
> a. Show that this is actually the case.
> b. Think up a number of other algebraic fraction that can be reduced to $\dfrac{x}{x+1}$.
>
> The more varied, the better!

FIGURE 4.6 Task to produce equivalent expressions (Kindt, 2011).

other examples of the same property, explicitly describe it and prove it. The final result is the "theorem" $(x + a)^2 - 1 = (x + a + 1)(x + a - 1)$. While procedural skills play an important role in this task, it also involves some production (thinking of more examples), pattern recognition, relating different properties and generalization, which are important aspects of school algebra that go beyond the purely procedural work. Proving the rule that is discovered may need some teacher guidance and may also be a suitable whole-class activity, answering the question "How can we be sure that this will always work?"

The fourth example task from Friedlander and Arcavi (2012; see Figure 4.7) is a classification task. It provides students with the freedom to design their own classification schemes. Different schemes can lead to interesting classroom discussions. An even more productive extension of the task would be to invite students to add other expressions to the collections and to either assign them to the existing classification or to extend the classification as well.

The four examples give a glimpse into the principles behind the idea of productive practice. The core element is that students experience some freedom, some room to create and to produce, rather than being caught in the designer's trap. Productive tasks invite reflection but in the meantime are grounded in skills which can be meaningfully practiced. In line with this, Friedlander and Arcavi (2012) offer an inventory of cognitive processes that can be addressed in productive practices, such as reverse thinking, constructing examples and counterexamples, and global comprehension. To design such productive tasks, Swan (2008) provides a list of design guidelines, such as the use of rich, collaborative tasks in which difficulties are confronted rather than avoided. Kindt (2011) summarizes his design principles in ten recommendations (see Figure 4.8), some of which are manifest in the four examples. For example, recommendation 1 clearly matches the idea of the first example on positioning brackets rather than expanding them. The second example on finding equivalent expressions reflects the second principle of task variation. It also involves a so-called "own production" (point 8). The notion of students' own productions was brought to the foreground by Treffers (1987) and comes down to inviting students to create their own tasks and exercises; such tasks may provide occasions for further practice by peer students, or the teacher may even invite students to design tasks that would be appropriate for a final written test. Once challenged in such a way, students may come up with creative examples of tasks. Why not exploit their creativity?

Classify the following expressions into two groups. Describe each group.

Classify the same expressions, this time into three groups. Describe each group.

$x^2 - 8x + 16$, $x^2 - 16$, $x^2 + 8x + 16$, $x^2 + 16$,
$x^2 - 10x + 25$, $x^2 + 25$, $x^2 - 25$, $x^2 + 10x - 25$,

FIGURE 4.7 Classification task (Friedlander & Arcavi, 2012).

> 1. Ask reverse questions to promote mental agility.
> 2. Vary the practice formats and activities as much as possible.
> 3. Challenge the students to reason logically (for example, by using coherent string of problems).
> 4. Challenge the students to generalize (for example, by means of number patterns).
> 5. Practice the substitution of "formulas in formulas" (formal substitution).
> 6. Practice the elimination of variables in systems of formulas or equations.
> 7. Pay attention to the verbal reading and writing of algebra rules or formulas.
> 8. Challenge the students to create their "own productions."
> 9. Also practice algebra in geometry.
>
> And more generally
> 10. Where possible, maintain and strengthen previously acquired computational and algebraic skills.

FIGURE 4.8 Principles of productive practice by Kindt (2011, p. 176).

To summarize this section, we conclude that a fluent mastery of procedural skills is important and requires practice. However, practice should not come down to just monotonously reproducing procedures until they have been automatized; this is not motivating for students, may even be counterproductive and creates skills that cannot adapt to slight variations. Rather, tasks should provide room for productive, insightful and challenging forms of practice, which show variation, which keep students alert and which appeal to creativity. The impact of such tasks, of course, also depends on the arrangement of the practice: individual, collaborative, using tools, in discussion, or different. The results of such tasks, which usually have more than one solution or strategy, can lead to lively and fruitful whole-class discussions in which student productions are synthesized and evaluated. While teaching, it can be efficient to use regular practicing tasks, for example from textbooks, but to include slight variations, to give them a more productive and challenging character.

4.4 The Reconciliation of Routine and Insight

In the previous section, a plea was made for productive practice, in which routine procedures and insight are integrated. As such, it relates to different views on the relationship between the two. It is this relationship, often the topic of debate, and its consequences for teaching algebra that will be addressed in this section.

Applying routine procedures is an important aspect of doing algebra. The fact that significant categories of problems can be solved through standardized procedures is a great intellectual achievement, acquired by the hard work of brilliant mathematicians over centuries; it reflects the power of algebra. Isn't it wonderful that problems such as solving linear equations, quadratic equations and systems of linear equations, or such as differentiating rational functions, can be accomplished in efficient and standardized ways that are guaranteed to provide the right answer in all cases, if the rules are followed correctly? In a linear equation in one variable, just move all terms containing variables to the left-hand side, and all constants to the right-hand side. For quadratic equations, just put them in a standard form and apply the quadratic formula. As indicated in Section 3.6, there is no need to put in much effort; energy can be saved for more interesting matters. It is important that students master these procedures so that they can experience the power of algebra. If not, they might suffer from too many distracting mistakes in routine algebra when they enter higher mathematics and its applications. Isn't the mastery of procedural skills, therefore, one of the main goals of algebra teaching?

Doing algebra, however, is more than just applying routine procedures. In some cases, the repertoire of standard procedures is not sufficient: variations from standard form may make it impossible to apply the standard procedures to a problem. What is the use of the mastery of algebraic procedures if one stands helpless when they cannot be applied directly? Also, future societal and professional needs will focus on flexible analytical reasoning skills, rather than on procedural skills that can be outsourced to online digital tools in which these procedures are automatized and encapsulated as algorithms (e.g., see Figure 4.9). Therefore, one might argue that the core goal of algebra education is the development of flexible strategic problem solving and reasoning skills, to be able to judge when the standard procedures do and do not apply. Isn't the danger of focusing on standard procedures, which are indeed part of the power of algebra, that it may obscure the insight into underlying algebraic meaning and hinder flexible problem solving?

Recently, a teacher recounted an experience that we expect will be recognized by many others. This teacher's 14-year-old students solved the equation $(x - 3)^2 + 5 = 30$ through expanding brackets, followed by applying the quadratic formula; no need to say that this was a cumbersome and error prone procedure. The 12-year-old students who entered the classroom for the next lesson and noticed this equation on the board, however, were immediately able to solve it through $(x - 3)^2 = 25$ and $x - 3 = 5$ or $x - 3 = -5$. Not knowing about quadratic equations, they could take a fresh look at the equation and see the straightforward solution strategy. Similar remarks can be made for the equation $(x - a)^5 = 32$. A routine approach to this problem would probably come down to expanding the brackets in the left-hand side. Even with a good mastery of procedural skills, this operation

Input interpretation:

| solve | $x^2 + 4x + p = 0$ | for | x |

Results:

$$x = -\sqrt{4 - p} - 2$$
$$x = \sqrt{4 - p} - 2$$

FIGURE 4.9 A digital tool for solving a quadratic equation containing a parameter (www.wolframalpha.com).

has the risk of calculation mistakes, and, even worse, this effort will not bring the student closer to the solution. And, finally, which experienced teacher does not recall seeing students expanding brackets and, as a next step, try to factorize the result?

This example illustrates the possible tension between automatization and insight; the caveat of "insight that is clogged by automatism" (Freudenthal, 1983, p. 469) can be avoided by providing tasks that do address practicing skills, but in the meantime appeal to the students' alertness, creativity and thinking. Of course, algebraic expertise includes both procedural fluency and algebraic insight. Being competent in school algebra implies, among other things, the opportunistic, flexible back-and-forth transition from routine actions (such as the automatic application of rules and procedures) to sense making (Arcavi, 2005). In other words, competence would include both the timely postponement of meaning in favor of quick and effective applications of procedures, but also, when necessary, desirable or when people "feel" it, the interruption of an automatic routine in order to question, reflect, conclude, relate ideas or create new meaning—or, to paraphrase Freudenthal's words, to unclog an automatism.

In algebra teaching, therefore, procedures should be linked to understanding of their meaning and to a flexible choice of solution methods; routine and insight go hand in hand and should be reconciled. As Friedlander and Arcavi (2012, p. 609) explain, the aim is that "rules, procedures, algorithms, sense making, meaningful reading, and the creation of algebraic expressions are thoroughly integrated into the learning process." The core question, therefore, is how to make this integration in algebra lessons happen and how to design and use tasks in class that connect these two aspects of algebraic expertise. Let us consider some examples.

As a first example we consider the so-called cover-up method, which offers a flexible approach to solving equations. Figure 4.10 shows this strategy implemented in an online applet. The first step to solve this equation—complex for many students—is to carefully inspect the equation to notice that we know something about the expression inside the bracket, which when raised to the third power yields 27. Therefore, we highlight it using the mouse. The applet repeats the expression on the next line, followed by the = sign. We see that, as the third power is 27, its value should be 3, which we type in. Next, we repeat this process of selecting a sub-expression and assigning a numerical value to it, until we find the value of x, in this case 12. Note that the transition from the second to the third equation would be harder if the numbers 12 and 3 are "less nice," for example, 7 and 5. This method is essentially that of undoing operations as described in Section 3.7. As explained there, it is flexible in the sense that it can be used for different types of equations, some of which may look quite complex. However, this method also has its limitations in that it can only be used for equations that are written in a form in which the variable appears only once. (See also Section 3.10 Task 11.) It is interesting to note that the two main conceptual elements in the strategy, namely the selection of an appropriate sub-expression and the assignment of its value, relate to the two available techniques in the applet, namely highlighting and entering numerical values. This is how the designer, Peter Boon, embedded

Emphases in Algebra Teaching   93

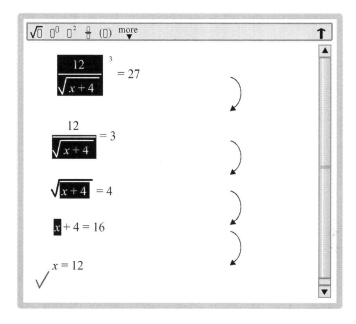

FIGURE 4.10 Solving a non-linear equation with the cover-up strategy (www.fisme.uu.nl/DWO/en).

didactical insights into the design of the applet. Research carried out by Jupri, Drijvers, and Van den Heuvel-Panhuizen (2014) suggests that this approach indeed improves students' equation solving skills.

As a second example, Figure 4.11 shows a task by Friedlander and Arcavi (2012). The interesting point here is that students are not asked to carry out the procedure, but to think about the result first. According to the authors, this is a useful strategy for predicting, monitoring and checking the validity of results—the latter being explicitly addressed by Pierce and Stacey (2004). Such types of qualitative thinking may help students to decide on strategies and next steps, and also empower them with means to detect mistakes and to monitor any work they do with digital tools such as computer algebra software.

A third type of task consists of including uncommon examples embedded in the well-known sequences of exercises that are common in many algebra textbooks. The column of exercises on the left of Figure 4.12 concerns quadratic equations. Once the students are familiar with the general quadratic formula, they may tend to always use it. However, item c in the sequence invites a more straightforward strategy, and the equation in task d isn't even a quadratic one. Similarly, the middle column is concerned with the differentiation of exponential functions. Once students get familiar with this, they may tend to ignore the fact that the third item is not exponential but cubic. As is the case in the left-hand column, working on such sets of exercises on the one hand aims at practicing procedural skills, but on the other hand also makes an appeal for an alert view on the equations and functions at stake.

94   Emphases in Algebra Teaching

Without multiplying the factors, predict the number of terms for each simplified product.

a. $(x + 8) \cdot (x - 6)$ d. $(x + 8) \cdot (y - 6)$

b. $(x + x) \cdot (8 - 6)$ e. $(x + y) \cdot (6 - 8)$

c. $(x + 8)^2$ f. $(x + 8) \cdot (x - 8)$

FIGURE 4.11   Prediction task (Friedlander & Arcavi, 2012).

Solve for x:	Find the derivative:	Find the derivative:
a. $x^2 + 3x + 2 = 0$	a. $f(x) = 2^x$	a. $g(x) = e^{2x}$
b. $x^2 + 3x + 1 = 0$	b. $f(x) = 3^x$	b. $h(x) = \sin(2x)$
c. $x^2 + 3x = 0$	c. $f(x) = x^3$	c. $m(x) = \ln(7x)$
d. $x + 3^2 = 0$	d. $f(x) = (1/3)^x$	d. $p(x) = \sqrt[3]{27x}$

FIGURE 4.12   Sequences of exercises with unusual elements.

The column of differentiation exercises on the right is somewhat different: it has an extension for those students who are already bored with practicing the chain rule: the task for them is to imagine that "the chain rule is broken" and to differentiate the given functions with other means. For example, $g(x)$ may be differentiated using the product rule, once rewritten as $g(x) = e^x \cdot e^x$, and the sum rule can be applied to m once simplified as $m(x) = \ln(x) + \ln(7)$. This activity will lead to the awareness that there may be different ways to find derivatives.

What these three types of examples share is a focus on a flexible insight in the problem solving strategy, and in what a sensible next step might be. Also, some flexibility is required, as well as a feeling for when to apply which procedure. To highlight the importance of insight into the affordances and constraints of routine procedures, and of flexible strategies, Fey (1990) introduced the notion of symbol sense, which was further elaborated by Arcavi (1994). Symbol sense is for algebra what number sense is for arithmetic: the flexible algebraic expertise that includes insight into the underlying concepts, the ability to give meaning to symbols, expressions and formulas, the feeling for their structure and the ability to "look through" them. Zorn (2002, p. 4) defines symbol sense as follows: "By symbol sense I mean a very general ability to extract mathematical meaning and structure from symbols, to encode meaning efficiently in symbols, and to manipulate symbols effectively to discover new mathematical meaning and structure."

What students need in the above examples is the algebraic insight to manage the complementary interplay between, on the one hand, skills in routine procedural work and, on the other hand, strategic insight into the value of these routines in a specific situation; a fresh look at problems and a mental "alarm alert system" that rings a bell in case experience indicates that routine is not enough. The art of algebra teaching lies in helping students to develop this type of symbol sense.

To summarize this section, we stress that considering routine and insight as opponents in algebra is not a sensible teaching approach. Rather, they represent two complementary faces of the same coin of algebraic expertise, both needed to fully exploit the power of algebra. Students should be able to carry out the procedural skills needed, and to use their insight and strategic skills to monitor the problem solving process and to switch to a more creative and flexible mode in non-standard situations. The flexible interplay of procedural skills and insight is both a main aim of teaching algebra and one of its main challenges.

As a teaching strategy for this aim, it makes sense to teach procedures so as to encourage them being applied flexibly. Also, tasks in which standard procedures are practiced may contain "surprising" non-standard variations, such as the ones presented in Figure 4.12. A teacher may invite students to explain why a certain method works, and in which cases it will not be useful. Strategies and inappropriate strategic choices may become a subject of classroom discussion.

4.5 Exploiting Student Mistakes

While doing algebra, students make mistakes. In some cases, such a mistake may be just a "slip of the pen" while carrying out a procedure, due to a lapse of concentration. In other cases, more serious reasons seem to be the underlying cause. Whatever the case, students may get frustrated by mistakes, as they drastically increase the time to finish the task and may make it more complex (or even more simple). Also, mistakes may affect students' self-confidence: "After so much practice, I am still unable to do this!" For teachers, noticing student mistakes may be frustrating as well, as they continue to re-appear in spite of the careful and patient explanations, the many examples and the time spent on practice in class. How can persistent mistakes be dealt with in algebra teaching?

Let us look at two frequent types of errors that students make and that are documented in the literature. The first type of error concerns the letter-as-object misconception addressed in Section 3.2. It comes down to students considering variables as standing for objects—persons, bananas, other things—instead of numbers. In the literature, this misconception is strongly associated with the Student-Professor problem, in which persons and numbers of persons are confused (e.g., see Rosnick, 1981), although other factors also play a role in this well-known task (MacGregor & Stacey, 1993). There are different teaching strategies to avoid the letter-as-object misconception. First, while introducing the notion of variable, it is very important to avoid too strong an association with the objects involved (as is done in "fruit salad algebra," see Section 3.2). This can be done by avoiding the use of letters associated with the objects, or by stressing that variables stand for numbers of objects, such as the number of wheels or the number of dollars to pay, etcetera. Second, the initial use of word formulas may help, and while doing so the use of extended variable names is recommended, for example:

Number_of_wheels = 4 x *Number_of_cars*

Of course, this is long-winded and invites abbreviated notations, but initially it makes sense to write such extended variable names. It may reduce the tendency to incorrectly translate "every car has four wheels" or "there are four wheels for every car" into the equations $c = 4w$ or $4w = c$. Third, it is wise to make students substitute test numbers in their equations, to see if they make sense. Fourth and final, it is good to make students aware of this type of error, so that they develop mental alarm bells that alert them to check for this error in cases that require this type of translation into algebra.

Another category of common mistakes concerns the following type of simplification:

$a^2 + b^2 = 49$ so $a + b = 7$. Wrong!

Or, similarly in the lens formula, which shows the relationship between the focal distance f of a lens, the object distance d and the image distance m:

$$\frac{1}{f} = \frac{1}{d} + \frac{1}{m} \text{ so } f = d + m. \text{ No!}$$

As a rationale or motivation for the first simplification, a student might believe that one can take the square root of a sum in a piece-wise manner. We are trapped in what De Bock and colleagues (2007) call the linearity illusion. For the first case this would come down to:

$$a + b = \sqrt{a^2} + \sqrt{b^2} = \sqrt{a^2 + b^2} = \sqrt{49} = 7. \text{ Mistake!}$$

Of course, the problem lies in the second equals sign: the square root of a sum is not equal to the sum of the partial square roots. Even though a teacher will get upset by this mistake, the student may be seeing an analogy with a problem in which a similar line of reasoning would work, namely with multiplication instead of addition and for positive values of a and b:

If $a^2 \times b^2 = 49$, then $a \times b = \sqrt{a^2} \times \sqrt{b^2} = \sqrt{a^2 \times b^2} = \sqrt{49} = 7$. Indeed!

Also, if we replace the operator "take the square root" by "multiply by 5," the trick works as well because five times the sum of squares is the sum of five times each of the squares:

$5(a^2 + b^2) = 5a^2 + 5b^2$

So students who make the first mistake in fact overgeneralize the distributive property of algebraic operations: multiplication does distribute over addition, and taking the square root distributes over multiplication, but not over addition! The lens formula example fails because the reciprocal operation does not distribute over addition. The distributive property has subtleties that are not easy to see through. In addition, the above simplification rules are very tempting because of their visual appearance in the formulas. Kirshner and Awtry (2004) call this the visual salience of a formula, which indeed may be difficult to resist.

To deal with this kind of difficulty, an appropriate teaching strategy might be to stress numerical substitution as a means to verify and to produce counterexamples. Indeed, when literal symbols and variables stand for numbers, algebraic properties and rules should be based on similar rules for numbers. So showing by calculation that $1^2 + 2^2$ does not equal $(1 + 2)^2$ might be helpful here; the same holds for:

$$\sqrt{2} = \sqrt{1+1} \neq \sqrt{1} + \sqrt{1} = 1+1 = 2$$

As for "$a^2 + b^2 = 49$ so $a + b = 7$," this could be shown to be false by drawing a right-angled triangle with a hypotenuse of length 7, and sides of length a and b, respectively. It is clear that $a + b$, the sum of two sides of the triangle, must be greater than 7.

Speaking in general, errors like these are resilient, difficult to eliminate, re-occur at unexpected moments, and many of them appear throughout different generations of students in different countries. They seem to be inherent to the way humans think about algebra. In teaching, they cannot be neglected. If we can't achieve all our students making errorless algebraic simplifications, let's make the best of it and consider addressing the underlying, often conceptual, causes of these mistakes. One way to do so is to turn the need into a virtue and to explicitly discuss such mistakes. Friedlander and Arcavi (2012) mention identifying errors and misconceptions as an important cognitive aspect of practice and recommend putting students in the position of teachers by studying the work by their (real or fictitious) peers. Requiring students to detect errors made by others can raise awareness of their own mistakes. This category of tasks enables teachers to select and discuss the kinds of mistakes they want to address (Friedlander & Arcavi, 2012). For example, Figure 4.13 provides a task in which students need to analyze the work of others to determine which answers are correct and to identify mistakes.

The mathematics teacher asked the class to substitute $a = 3$ in
$$-5 - \frac{3+2a}{3}$$
Check the work of the following students and make the necessary corrections.

Abe $\quad -5 - \dfrac{3+6}{3} = -5 - 1 + 6 = 0$

Benjamin $\quad -5 - \dfrac{3+6}{3} = \dfrac{-15 - 3 + 6}{3} = \dfrac{-12}{3} = 4$

Claire $\quad -5 - \dfrac{3+6}{3} = -5 - \dfrac{9}{3} = -8$

Diana $\quad -5 - \dfrac{3+6}{3} = -5 - \dfrac{9}{3} = -2$

FIGURE 4.13 Students detecting errors (Friedlander & Arcavi, 2012, p. 612).

98 Emphases in Algebra Teaching

A similar approach is followed in the task shown in Figure 4.14. In addition to these tasks, a teacher might even go further by challenging students to show convincing and tempting mistakes on purpose, and explain both why they are tempting and why they are wrong. The teacher might discuss the reasons for the errors, whilst being careful not to promote memory of the bad over the good.

To summarize this section, it is well known that student mistakes in algebraic procedures are persistent. Some are just "slips of the pen" and will be immediately recognized as such by the student, once they are pointed out. Other mistakes, however, have a conceptual background, and may reflect a misconception, a limited insight into the meaning of an operation or an overgeneralization. They may have foundations that are worthwhile considering.

In teaching, these mistakes and misconceptions should not be neglected, but rather should be taken seriously. As a teacher, one may try to uncover and discuss the rationale behind them. In this sense, mistakes are obstacles but also opportunities for learning. They are also opportunities for the teacher as well, because mistakes may reflect omissions in the teaching process. An appropriate teaching strategy may consist of offering productive tasks that provide construction room to students and invite students' flexibility, as described in Section 4.3. A second strategy is to avoid mistakes by connecting syntactical rules to meaningful models, such as the balance model for solving equations explained in Section 3.7 (see also Tabach, Hershkowitz, & Arcavi, 2008). A third teaching guideline is to explicitly address mistakes and use them as springboards for mathematical exploration rather than considering them as an unwelcome disruption of the intended teaching (Borasi, 1987).

Simplify: $\dfrac{y^2+7y+6}{y^2+8y+12}$

One student tackles the problem as follows. The first step is to cancel out y^2 in the numerator and denominator:

$$\dfrac{7y+6}{8y+12}$$

After this he subtracted $7y$ from the numerator and denominator:

$$\dfrac{6}{y+12}$$

Then he subtracted the 6 in the numerator from the 12 in the denominator. Nothing remains in the numerator, so it disappears. So the answer is:

$$y+6$$

The student made several mistakes. What are the mistakes and why are they wrong?

FIGURE 4.14 Explicitly addressing mistakes (Drijvers, Goddijn, & Kindt, 2011, p. 21).

Fourth and final, it can be fruitful to refer to the underlying meanings of the algebraic procedures, for example:

- In the case of the letter-as-object category, refer to variables as standing for numbers, and stimulate numerical substitution as a means to verify algebraic relations.
- In the case of the distributive property example, refer to algebraic properties as extended arithmetical properties.
- In other cases, refer to underlying models that may have been forgotten, such as the balance model for solving equations, or the rectangular area model for expanding brackets (see Figure 4.1).

4.6 Proofs in Algebra Teaching

Proofs are at the heart of mathematics, not just of geometry, where they usually have an important role, but also of algebra, where proofs are needed to check the truth of conjectures and properties. Proving is not only intellectually rewarding, it also empowers us with the certainty that a theorem or rule is a valid consequence of other rules. Not including proofs as an important element in algebra teaching would not do justice to the character of mathematics, and it would also deprive students of experiencing the power of algebra. Also, if critical thinking is among one of the goals of contemporary mathematics education, we should not train our students to just believe what we say. Therefore, proving is identified as one of the aims of algebra education in Chapter 1.

Teachers may decide not to provide proofs in algebra education for different reasons. One reason may be that the focus of the course is on algebra in applications and modeling, and proofs are considered not to fit in well. Another reason may be that proofs are considered to make a limited contribution to students' understanding. A third reason can be that proofs are seen as too abstract and too hard for the students. Even if one can understand these arguments, not paying attention to proof would deprive students from experiencing the power of generalization in algebra. Therefore, one of the challenges of algebra teaching is to help students experience proof, and the reasoning and certainty involved, in ways that do contribute to purposeful and meaningful algebra and, in the meantime, are within the scope of the students.

In this chapter, we have already seen some examples of algebraic proofs. For example, the rod-and-beams formulas of Figure 4.2 can be proved to be equivalent through the application of rules to rewrite them (or indeed by noting that they all describe the same practical situation). Also, expanding $a^2 - (a + 1) \times (a - 1)$ will prove the patterns discovered in calculations like $2 \times 2 - 1 \times 3$, $3 \times 3 - 2 \times 4$, $4 \times 4 - 5 \times 3$, etcetera, which are addressed in Section 4.2. In the example presented in Figure 4.4, algebra is used to prove that a geometrical property appearing on the screen is not a matter of coincidence, but is always exactly true.

We now focus on just one example of students' experiencing proof in algebra. It concerns the formula for the solutions of quadratic equations. In some countries, this rule is just presented to students as an easy trick that they should take on the authority of their teacher and just use. Graphing calculators provide programs to apply the rule, so who complains? Of course, a top-down whole-class demonstration of the proof by the teacher is cumbersome for many students. But couldn't it be taught in a way that provokes more student engagement? For example, let us assume that students are familiar with the technique of completing the square. Also, they know the quadratic formula. Figure 4.15 shows a table with pairs of formulas and next steps to be taken to form a proof. Now the teacher may cut the table into horizontal strips. In an attempt to prove the formula, (groups of) students are asked to put them in the correct order. A second and more difficult approach would be to also cut the strips vertically, so that the formulas and the step descriptions are also separated. This can also be organized in a whole-class setting, with one student moving texts and formulas on an interactive whiteboard, in interaction with other students (Figure 4.16). A third, even harder way would be to provide students with the first and the last formula shown in Figure 4.15, and with all the step descriptions from the second column. The task in this case would be to make a chain of step descriptions from the first formula to the end formula, and to complete the intermediate steps by hand. A fourth approach, for gifted students, would be to just provide them with the first and the final formula, and invite them to get from the one to the other by completing the square. As soon as they get stuck, the teacher provides them with the step description that matches the phase of their solution process. An easier approach, finally, is to provide students with the horizontal slices of the table shown in Figure 4.15, but this time with numbers instead of the parameters a, b and c. If different groups solve the equations for different parameter values, a whole-class discussion might lead to a general description, and eventually to the general formula. Of course, the use of the absolute value in step 7 is subtle and may need a further discussion.

To summarize this section, proof is an indispensable part of algebra. Even if proofs may be perceived as abstract and formal by the students, the challenge for teachers is to find means to address the key ideas of proofs and proving in ways that involve students and make the property or theory to be proved more purposeful and meaningful to them.

Formula	Description of the next step
$ax^2 + bx + c = 0$	Multiply by a ($a \neq 0$)
$(ax)^2 + abx + ac = 0$	Complete the square for ax
$\left(ax + \dfrac{b}{2}\right)^2 - \dfrac{b^2}{4} + ac = 0$	Isolate the squared term
$\left(ax + \dfrac{b}{2}\right)^2 = \dfrac{b^2 - 4ac}{4}$	Take the square root, supposing $b^2 - 4ac \geq 0$
$ax + \dfrac{b}{2} = -\sqrt{\dfrac{b^2 - 4ac}{4}}$ or $ax + \dfrac{b}{2} = \sqrt{\dfrac{b^2 - 4ac}{4}}$	Isolate x
$x = -\dfrac{b + \sqrt{b^2 - 4ac}}{2a}$ or $x = -\dfrac{b - \sqrt{b^2 - 4ac}}{2a}$	Ready, solved!

FIGURE 4.15 Ingredients for a proof of the quadratic formula.

$ax + \dfrac{b}{2} = -\sqrt{\dfrac{b^2 - 4ac}{4}}$ or $ax + \dfrac{b}{2} = \sqrt{\dfrac{b^2 - 4ac}{4}}$	
	Take the square root, supposing $b^2 - 4ac \geq 0$
	Isolate x
	$x = -\dfrac{b + \sqrt{b^2 - 4ac}}{2a}$ or $x = -\dfrac{b - \sqrt{b^2 - 4ac}}{2a}$
$\left(ax + \dfrac{b}{2}\right)^2 - \dfrac{b^2}{4} + ac = 0$	
Isolate the square term	$ax^2 + bx + c = 0$
	Ready, solved!
$\left(ax + \dfrac{b}{2}\right)^2 = \dfrac{b^2 - 4ac}{4}$	Complete the square for ax
	$(ax)^2 + abx + ac = 0$
Multiply by a ($a \neq 0$)	

FIGURE 4.16 Slide for a whole-class proof of the quadratic formula using an interactive whiteboard.

4.7 Chapter Summary

This chapter took a teaching perspective on algebra education and included the following key points. In Section 4.2 we highlighted that teaching algebra in context is important to emphasize the purpose and meaning of algebra to students. Authentic problem situations and real life contexts may be useful, as long as they are not artificial. For older or more advanced students, abstract problem situations (e.g., from the world of numbers or from geometry) may serve as appropriate entrances to or applications of algebra as well. Appropriate tasks may be found in online repositories (see suggestions in the next section).

In Section 4.3, a key point is that practice need not come down to monotonously reproducing procedures to reach for automatization. Tasks in which students produce rather than just reproduce, and thus experience the productive power of algebra, are at the same time challenging and integrate the practice for routine as well as insight building. Such tasks may be exploited in lively and fruitful whole-class discussions. Variations in types of tasks and in ways to practice are recommended.

In Section 4.4 we stress that routine procedural fluency and algebraic insight are not opponents in algebra. Rather, they represent two complementary faces of the same coin of algebraic expertise, both needed to fully exploit the power of algebra. Students should be able to carry out the routine procedural skills needed, but also be able to monitor the problem solving process and to switch to a more creative and flexible mode in non-standard situations. These are two challenging aspects of teaching algebra that make appeals for creativity not only on the part of the student, but also on the part of the teacher. Tasks that contain "surprising" non-standard variations may help here.

Difficulties with algebraic manipulation, and corresponding mistakes, are always with us and can hardly be avoided. Section 4.5, therefore, highlights a key point in the art of algebra teaching: the ability to deal with such mistakes in a fruitful way. Neglecting mistakes or considering them as unexpected disruptions to the learning process may not be an appropriate teaching strategy. Rather, we recommend taking mistakes as opportunities to investigate underlying concepts and to re-address conceptual models that may prevent the mistakes re-appearing.

Proof, finally, is an indispensable part of algebra. Even though proofs may be perceived as abstract and formal by students, we claim in Section 4.6 that proofs and proving may help students to experience the power of algebra and to better understand the property that they have proven. Again, the challenge for teachers is to find means to address the key ideas of proofs in accessible ways that involve students.

4.8 Thinking Further

Section 4.2 Teaching Algebra in Context

1. In Section 4.2, a plea is made for problem situations that form meaningful starting points for different topics in the algebra curriculum. Examine some of the problem situations in algebra chapters in textbooks. Discuss their authenticity in terms of meaning and purpose. Try to find problem situations that would be appropriate to start the teaching of equations, or of another topic that you will be teaching soon.
2. Visit some educational resources (e.g., the website of the Ritemaths project https://extranet.education.unimelb.edu.au/DSME/RITEMATHS/general_access/curriculum_resources/quadratic_functions/index.shtml) and look for a meaningful and authentic task on quadratic functions.
3. For experiencing the meaning and purpose of algebra, structuring a (sub) domain may help students to perceive its position within the "world of algebra." For quadratics, such an overview is provided in https://extranet.education.unimelb.edu.au/DSME/RITEMATHS/general_access/curriculum_resources/quadratic_functions/index.shtml. Look at this overview. Choose a domain, e.g., equations or function, and design a similar overview of the types of objects and the corresponding algebraic procedures to structure its "landscape," for example in the form of a mind map. If you

have an algebra class, discuss this landscape with your students, or, even better, set up such a landscape in a whole-class discussion.

Section 4.3 Productive Practice

4. In Section 4.3 it is recommended to offer productive and surprising tasks that aim at both procedural fluency and insight, that invite students to discover patterns and interesting phenomena, or that beg for deeper thinking and proof. Visit Kindt's (2004) online collection of productive tasks, choose some tasks, decide why they are productive (or not) and use some of them in your algebra class.
5. To harvest the results from practicing tasks such as the ones addressed in Section 4.3, whole-class discussions are indispensable. Choose some tasks and think of ways to discuss the main lessons learnt from them with your class. If possible, try to make such whole-class discussion happen and reflect on its impact after the lesson. Discuss your experiences with your colleagues.

Section 4.4 The Reconciliation of Routine and Insight

6. As described in Section 4.4, routine and insight are partners in algebra. Visit the Ritemaths website (https://extranet.education.unimelb.edu.au/DSME/RITEMATHS/general_access/research_materials/research_index.shtml) and download the Algebra Expectation Quiz (or see Ball, Pierce & Stacey, 2003). Try it in your class and reflect about its results with your colleagues.

Section 4.5 Exploiting Student Mistakes

7. To help students develop insight into the structure of algebraic expressions and to avoid the type of errors described in Section 4.5, offer them "algebra dictations" in which the task is to write down algebraic symbols that reflect phrases the teacher reads aloud in natural language, e.g., "the sum of the squares of a and b." Design some phrases for such an algebra dictation and, if possible, try this in one of your classrooms.

Section 4.6 Proofs in Algebra Teaching

8. Section 4.6 highlights the importance of proof. Detecting a mistake in a proof can also be a challenge, addressed in an individual activity, in group work or in a whole-class discussion. How about the following one?

   Theorem: There are no prime numbers bigger than 19.
   "Proof":
   Suppose $n > 19$.
   If n is even, it is not prime, done.

If n is odd, then $\dfrac{n+1}{2}$ and $\dfrac{n-1}{2}$ are natural numbers.

Thus, the following equality holds: $n = \left(\dfrac{n+1}{2}\right)^2 - \left(\dfrac{n-1}{2}\right)^2$

The latter expression is of the form $n = a^2 - b^2 = (a-b)(a+b)$

So we expressed n as a product of two factors, and therefore it is not prime!

4.9 References

Ainley, J., Bills, L., & Wilson, K. (2005). Designing spreadsheet-based tasks for purposeful algebra. *International Journal of Computers for Mathematical Learning, 10*(3), 191–215.

Arcavi, A. (1994). Symbol sense: Informal sense-making in formal mathematics. *For the Learning of Mathematics, 14*(3), 24–35.

Arcavi, A. (2005). Developing and using symbol sense in mathematics. *For the Learning of Mathematics, 25*(2), 42–47.

Ball, L., Pierce, R., & Stacey, K. (2003). Recognising equivalent algebraic expressions: An important component of algebraic expectation for working with CAS. In N. A. Pateman, B. J. Dougherty and J. T. Zillox (Eds.), *Proceedings of the 27th Annual Conference of the International Group for the Psychology of Mathematics Education, Vol. 4* (pp. 15–22). Hawaii: University of Hawaii. http://files.eric.ed.gov/fulltext/ED501048.pdf (accessed September 7, 2015).

Baumert, J., Kunter, M., Blum, W., Brunner, M., Voss, T., Jordan, A., et al. (2010). Teachers' mathematical knowledge, cognitive activation in the classroom, and student progress. *American Educational Research Journal, 47*(1), 133–180.

Borasi, R. (1987). Exploring mathematics through the analysis of errors. *For the Learning of Mathematics, 7*(3), 2–8.

De Bock, D., Van Dooren, W., Janssens, D., & Verschaffel, L. (2007). *Illusion of Linearity: From Analysis to Improvement.* New York: Springer.

Drijvers, P., Dekker, T., & Wijers, M. (2011). Patterns and formulas. In P. Drijvers (Ed.), *Secondary Algebra Education. Revisiting Topics and Themes and Exploring the Unknown* (pp. 89–100). Rotterdam: Sense.

Drijvers, P., Goddijn, A., & Kindt, M. (2011). Algebra education: Exploring topics and themes. In P. Drijvers (Ed.), *Secondary Algebra Education. Revisiting Topics and Themes and Exploring the Unknown* (pp. 5–26). Rotterdam, Boston, Taipei: Sense Publishers.

Fey, J. T. (1990). Quantity. In L. A. Steen (Ed.), *On the Shoulders of Giants* (pp. 61–94). Washington D.C.: National Academy Press.

Freudenthal, H. (1983). *Didactical Phenomenology of Mathematical Structures.* Dordrecht: Reidel Publishing Company.

Freudenthal, H. (1991). *Revisiting Mathematics Education.* China Lectures. Dordrecht: Kluwer Academic Publishers.

Friedlander, A., & Arcavi, A. (2012). How to practice it: An integrated approach to algebraic skills. *Mathematics Teacher, 105*(8), 608–614.

Jupri, A., Drijvers, P., & Van den Heuvel-Panhuizen, M. (2014). Student difficulties in solving equations from an operational and a structural perspective. *Mathematics Education, 9*(1), 39–55.

Kindt, M. (2004). *Positive Algebra. A Collection of Productive Exercises*. Utrecht: Freudenthal Institute. www.primas-project.eu/servlet/supportBinaryFiles?referenceId=4&supportId =1526 (accessed September 7, 2015).

Kindt, M. (2011). Principles of practice. In P. Drijvers (Ed.), *Secondary Algebra Education. Revisiting Topics and Themes and Exploring the Unknown* (pp. 137–178). Rotterdam: Sense.

Kirshner, D., & Awtry, T. (2004). Visual salience of algebraic transformations. *Journal for Research in Mathematics Education, 35*(4), 224–257.

Li, S. (1999). Does practice make perfect? *For the Learning of Mathematics, 19*(3), 33–35.

Lockwood, E. H. (1961). *A Book of Curves*. Cambridge: Cambridge University Press. www.aproged.pt/biblioteca/ABookofCurvesLockwood.pdf (accessed September 7, 2015).

MacGregor, M., & Stacey, K. (1993). Cognitive models underlying students' formulation of simple linear equations. *Journal for Research in Mathematics Education, 24*, 217–232.

Mason, J. (2005). *Developing Thinking in Algebra*. London: The Open University.

Niss, M., Blum, W., & Galbraith, P. (2007). Introduction. In W. Blum, P. Galbraith, H-W. Henn & M. Niss (Eds.), (2007). *Modelling and Applications in Mathematics Education. The 14th ICMI Study* (pp. 3–32). New York, NY: Springer Science + Business Media, LLC.

Pierce, R., & Stacey, K. (2004). A framework for monitoring progress and planning teaching towards effective use of computer algebra systems. *International Journal of Computers for Mathematical Learning, 9*(1), 59–93.

Rosnick, P. (1981). Some misconceptions concerning the concept of a variable. *Mathematics Teacher, 74*(6), 418–420.

Shulman, L. S. (1987). Knowledge and teaching: Foundations of the new reform. *Harvard Educational Review, 57*(1), 1–22.

Swan, M. (2008). A Designer Speaks. *Educational Designer, 1*(1). www.educationaldesigner.org/ed/volume1/issue1/article3/ (accessed September 7, 2015).

Tall, D., & Thomas, M. (1991). Encouraging versatile thinking in algebra using the computer. *Educational Studies in Mathematics, 22*, 125–147.

Tabach, M., Hershkowitz, R., & Arcavi, A. (2008). Learning beginning algebra with spreadsheets in a computer intensive environment. *Journal of Mathematical Behavior, 27*, 48–63.

Treffers, A. (1987). *Three Dimensions. A Model of Goal and Theory Description in Mathematics Instruction – The Wiskobas Project*. Dordrecht: D. Reidel Publishing Company.

Van den Heuvel-Panhuizen, M., & Drijvers, P. (2013). Realistic mathematics education. In S. Lerman (Ed.), *Encyclopedia of Mathematics Education*. Dordrecht, Heidelberg, New York, London: Springer.

Wijers, M., Roodhardt, A., Reeuwijk, M. van, Dekker, T., Burrill, G., Cole, B. R., & Pligge, M. A. (2006). Building formulas. In Wisconsin Center for Education Research & Freudenthal Institute (Eds.), *Mathematics in Context*. Chicago, USA: Encyclopedia Britannica Inc.

Zorn, P. (2002). *Algebra, Computer Algebra and Mathematical Thinking*. Contribution to the 2nd International Conference on the Teaching of Mathematics, 2002, Hersonissos, Crete. www.stolaf.edu/people/zorn/cretepaper.pdf (accessed September 7, 2015).

5

ALGEBRA EDUCATION IN THE DIGITAL ERA

> Technology is an essential tool for learning mathematics in the 21st century, and all schools must ensure that all their students have access to technology. Effective teachers maximize the potential of technology to develop students' understanding, stimulate their interest, and increase their proficiency in mathematics. When technology is used strategically, it can provide access to mathematics for all students.
> (National Council of Teachers of Mathematics, 2008, p. 1)

5.1 Introduction

In the previous chapters, algebraic activity is characterized by actions of representing and manipulating core algebraic objects such as variable, expression, equation, function and graph. The perspectives of beginning learners and teachers have been addressed. An aspect that has not been addressed so far, however, is that we live in a digital era. Nowadays, the world around us is full of technological tools. Digital devices such as smartphones and tablets play important roles in our daily lives and offer immediate access to information and continuous means for connectivity and communication. Distant collaboration among students or between teacher and students is feasible. Massive open online courses (MOOCs) and online textbook series are getting widespread. The natural question, then, is how this immersion may affect education. In addition to communications facilities and general purpose applications, dedicated cognitive tools for doing and learning mathematics are available. Will schools be isolated islands in which students are deprived of their digital tools? Do new media and technologies impact on curricular goals? For example, are factual knowledge and by-hand skills losing importance? Can teaching and learning processes be improved by the integration of digital technology?

In the present chapter, this general issue is addressed for the case of algebra education. Calculators, computers and smartphone apps offer substantial mathematical functionality and algebraic power, such as spreadsheets, equation solvers and graphing tools in which the users only need enter input to carry out algebraic procedures (e.g., see the Wolfram Alpha example in Figure 4.9). Schools are equipped with digital tools, and in many countries students are allowed to use some of these in assessments and examinations.

The core question, therefore, is: how is digital technology changing algebra education, including both its curricular content goals and its teaching and learning practices? What are the challenges that digital tools pose to teachers, curriculum developers and teaching material designers? What opportunities do digital tools offer to algebra education, and how can they be exploited when new algebra teaching practices are strongly supported by digital tools?

Concerning the curricular goals of algebra, the availability of sophisticated digital tools raises fundamental questions. Why teach algebraic proficiency if your smartphone has a graphing app that shows you the zeros of your function and provides access to a website which "does algebra" (see Figure 4.9)? Which algebraic skills and knowledge should be at the heart of contemporary algebra curricula? Although the debate is an ongoing one, the overall opinion seems to be that the basic concepts of algebra are still central. To master these concepts, a certain amount of pen-and-paper experience is needed to acquire algebraic proficiency, that also is needed while using a powerful digital algebra tool. Pen-and-paper skills, mastery of digital tools and conceptual understanding are intertwined and hard to unravel. We believe that digital tools for algebra raise questions about curricular goals. In the meantime we see some elementary "old school" pen-and-paper algebraic proficiency as indispensable for experiencing the "feel and touch" of algebra and, as such, for the insight into the broad underlying principles related to algebraic structure.

Meanwhile, we see gradual curricular and pedagogical changes. For example, investigating functions in the mechanistic way of finding domain, range, zeros, extreme values, asymptotes, to finally be able to draw a graph, which was common practice some decades ago, nowadays receives less attention thanks to the availability of graphing technology. Rather, functions may be presented through digital means in a more dynamic way, through which co-variation of independent and dependent variables is explored. For example, Figure 5.1 shows four isosceles triangles with two sides of length 5. Digital technology, in this case dynamic geometry software, enables students to experience the functional relationship between the area and the central angle in a visual and dynamic environment, and to simultaneously observe the graph of this function. Students make conjectures and have to use algebraic models and some knowledge of geometry to either prove or reject them (Arcavi & Hadas, 2000).

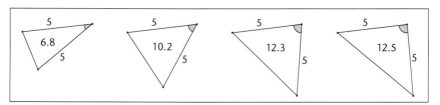

FIGURE 5.1 Exploring the area of an isosceles triangle as a function of its central angle (adapted from Arcavi & Hadas, 2000).

This example shows that digital tools allow for explorative and even guess–check–improve approaches. Other examples of this approach include the task of finding a symbolic expression for a graph, with graphical feedback providing the chance to improve it if not yet correct (e.g., see the early Green Globs game described in Dugdale, 1993, or Ruthven, 1990). Digital tools also allow for re-sequencing algebra education (Heid, 1988). This evolution of curricular goals and corresponding teaching approaches in algebra education is an ongoing one; the appropriate balance between traditional pen-and-paper skills and technology-supported algebraic activity is a delicate one.

To address the impact of digital tools on algebra education, we will first draw up a global inventory of the landscape of relevant digital tools, which leads to the identification of some overarching characteristics and dimensions (Section 5.2). In Section 5.3, we focus on the different kinds of opportunities digital tools offer for algebra education in general and for the teaching of the core concepts of variable, equation and function in particular. In Section 5.4, we reflect on these examples from a more theoretical perspective. In Sections 5.5 and 5.6, we summarize the chapter's key points and provide suggestions for further thinking.

5.2 Digital Tools for Algebra

Digital technologies are used more and more in education. From a hardware perspective, many teachers use Interactive White Boards (IWB) or digital projectors that allow the use of all kinds of internet resources and software and the benefit of interactive and dynamic teaching. Some schools provide desktop computers, and students may come with their own devices, such as graphing calculators, smartphones, tablets and laptop computers. However, the borders between handheld and desktop devices are getting fuzzy, as graphing calculators are getting more powerful, and tablets and smartphones offer more and more mathematical applications. Therefore, in spite of the important practical implications of the actual type of hardware for its use in the classroom, we focus on the tool's affordances for algebra rather than the physical size and appearance of the device in use.

From a software perspective, there are general-purpose tools that may be used for communication and for the distribution of mathematical content. Teachers may use their IWB or digital projector to display the textbook and its interactive components, or may use slide shows in their lessons. For students, online repositories and applications (applets) can provide exercises and offer feedback, possibly embedded in a learning management system that allows the teacher to monitor students' performance. Also, collections of video clips are available online, that offer explanations of content and support "blended learning," a teaching and learning approach that combines face-to-face classroom methods with computer mediated activities and "flipped classroom" strategies, in which instructional content is delivered online outside of the classroom (e.g., see www.khanacademy.org/). Even more sophisticated are online courses (e.g., massive open online courses or MOOCs) that integrate explanatory video clips, interactive tasks, collaboration among students and interaction with teachers.

5.2.1 Algebraic Functionality of Digital Tools

More specifically for algebra, a myriad of digital tools is available, in handheld or desktop software or through the internet. Some are quite open and versatile, whereas others are dedicated to specific educational purposes. For teachers, it may be hard to decide which tool to use when. To somewhat organize the wide landscape of Information and Communication Technology (ICT) tools for algebra education and to help in making such decisions, we distinguish two main dimensions, one on algebraic functionality and one on the pedagogical role. Within the algebraic functionality dimension, we distinguish four main categories: symbolic functionality, graphing functionality, table functionality, and visualization and representation functionality.

Let us first address *symbolic functionality*. As symbolic representations are central in algebra, a digital tool for algebra education should provide the functionality to properly deal with variable, expressions and equations, and algebraic manipulations on them. A crucial requirement, of course, is the possibility to enter formulas and expressions in a user-friendly way. Correct entry is one aspect of digital use where symbol sense is essential, e.g., to distinguish e—the letter or a variable name—from e, the base of the natural logarithm.

A first means to enter a symbolic representation is through a graphical equation editor, available in most software for algebra. This has its own peculiar character and therefore requires some specific practice. For example, while entering $y = \sqrt{5}x$ one should take care not to enter $y = \sqrt{5x}$ (see Figure 5.2).

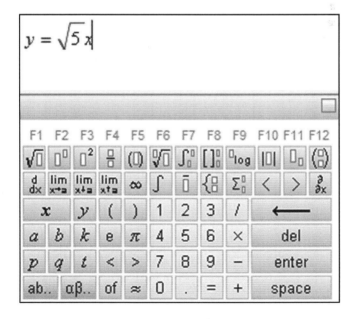

FIGURE 5.2 Entering an expression using an equation editor.

A second means to enter symbolic expressions is through sequential line entry. An example, shown in the upper left part of Figure 5.3, is $(x\wedge2 + 1)\wedge(1/2)$. The software, in this case Wolfram Alpha, displays the input in two-dimensional, pretty graphical format (bottom left part), which facilitates the verification of the input. This way of entering expressions usually requires the use of additional symbols such as ^ for superscripts, and careful use of brackets. As a consequence, it is not straightforward for students. As a third way to enter symbolic expressions, handwriting recognition is a promising development (see Figure 5.3 right part).

The most powerful and sophisticated symbolic functionality can be found in computer algebra systems (CAS), which offer a whole range of algebraic features. Figure 5.4 shows some randomly selected examples, with the user input on the left-hand side of each of the lines, and the software output on the right-hand side. The examples concern algebraic substitution, fraction addition, equation solving, and expansion and factorization. It is important to notice that the CAS does not reproduce the answers from a library of tasks, but really has the algorithms on board to evaluate whatever example the user had in mind. CAS is available in both commercial and open source form, and for handheld and desktop devices. In some countries students have CAS at their disposal during examinations and tests. CAS may also run in the background, as a mathematical engine behind educational software that evaluates student responses and offers feedback without the user being aware of its role (Sangwin, 2013).

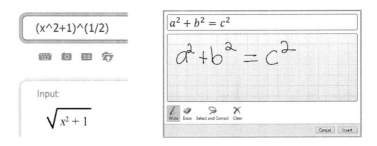

FIGURE 5.3 Automated recognition of line entry (left) and of handwritten input (right).

$x^2 + x \mid x = 3$	12
$\text{comDenom}(\dfrac{1}{p} + \dfrac{1}{q})$	$\dfrac{p+q}{pq}$
solve $(x + \sqrt{x} - 2 = 0, x)$	$x = 1$
expand $((a + b)^3)$	$a^3 + 3a^2b + 3ab^2 + b^3$
factor $(a^3 + 3a^2b + 3ab^2 + b^3)$	$(a + b)^3$

FIGURE 5.4 Symbolic functionality of CAS software.

Algebra Education in the Digital Era   **111**

The second type of functionality, *graphing functionality*, comes down to the opportunity to use the digital tool to graph functions. Graphing calculators, of course, do the job for you, and function graphers for computers or tablets offer the advantages of a larger screen. An important advantage of this graphing functionality compared to pen-and-paper graphing is that the digital graphs can be manipulated, i.e., one can easily change the window, zoom in, trace points or change the formula. The ease of graphing also opens new means of understanding functions, solving equations and investigating the impact of a parameter value in a formula.

Graphs may invite algebraic thinking. As an example, Figure 5.5 contains a GeoGebra screen that shows the graphs of two linear functions f and g with $f(x) = a \cdot x + b$ and $g(x) = c \cdot x + d$, as well as the graph of the product function h defined by $h(x) = f(x) \cdot g(x)$. The task—or in this case we might say the game—is to manipulate the graph of h indirectly by changing the values of the parameters a, b, c and/or d with the slider bars in the upper-right corner. Different questions can be raised. For example, for what values of the parameters will the parabola be opened upwards? Under which conditions will it touch the horizontal axis? What relationship will hold if the parabola's vertex lies vertically above or below the intersection point of the two lines? These questions can be answered experimentally in the graphing environment: the graphing tool provides the means for empirical work that supports conjecturing and generalizing, and finally may invite algebraic proofs!

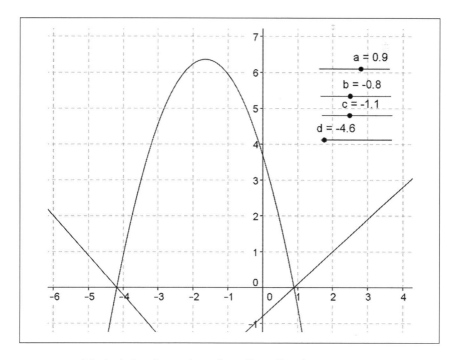

FIGURE 5.5   Manipulating the product of two linear functions.

Table functionality involves the opportunity to make tables of values for given algebraic relationships or functions. Spreadsheet software such as Excel has this functionality as its central option; other tools, such as graphing calculators, also offer this feature, and in addition have a more accessible way to set the step size to create tables of values of defined functions. As is the case for graphs, tables can also invite algebra. For example, Figure 5.6 (top) shows the table of a quadratic function f for input values of x ranging from 1 to 9. Several tasks emerge. One is to reconstruct the formula for $f(x)$. Another one would be to change this formula and to investigate the effect on the values of g and h. Is there a pattern? Can you prove with algebra that for all quadratic functions f, the function g will be linear? And h will be constant? The bottom part of Figure 5.6 shows an algebraic verification using a computer algebra tool, in this case from GeoGebra. The function f is defined with a general quadratic formula. Function g is the difference function of f and the calculation shows it to be linear in x. Function h, finally, is the difference function of g and, therefore, the second difference of f. Indeed, it is constant, and the value depends only on the coefficient of x^2 in the definition of f. Please note the analogue with the second derivative of a quadratic function being constant! The application of the CAS clearly requires students to know what they are doing and to be able to "talk in the language of functions." Also, they need to be able to interpret answers, e.g., to understand what it means when $h(x) = 2a$. The combination of the table functionality and the symbolic functionality here turns out to be very powerful for fostering algebraic insight and symbol sense.

Of course, symbols, graphs and tables can all represent mathematical functions and relationships. The fourth functionality preludes to the pedagogical use of ICT and concerns *visualization and representation*. It refers not only to the opportunity to use multiple representations and combine them, but also to use other, more dedicated, representations available in some pedagogical software

x	1	2	3	4	5	6	7	8	9
$f(x)$	4	8	18	34	56	84	118	158	204
$g(x) = f(x+1) - f(x)$	4	10	16	22	28	34	40	46	
$h(x) = g(x+1) - g(x)$	6	6	6	6	6	6	6		

$f(x) := a^* x \wedge 2 + b^*x + c$
$\rightarrow f(x) := a x^2 + b x + c$

$g(x) := f(x+1) - f(x)$
$\rightarrow g(x) := 2 a x + a + b$

$h(x) := g(x+1) - g(x)$
$\rightarrow h(x) := 2 a$

FIGURE 5.6 Function values and first and second order differences (Excel) and a general verification through computer algebra (GeoGebra).

Algebra Education in the Digital Era **113**

(Yerushalmy & Swidan, 2012). Examples are representing a variable as an empty box, an expression as a tree, an equation as a balance (see Figure 3.11), a function as an arrow chain (see Figure 3.9) or a product as a rectangle (see Figure 2.8). Figure 5.7 shows a digital tool called Algebra Arrows (Doorman, Drijvers, Gravemeijer, Boon, & Reed, 2012) in which students can set up arrow chain representations of the functions, in this case to transform temperatures in degrees Fahrenheit into temperatures in degrees Celsius. This reflects the "instructions for a process" view on expressions and functions described in Section 3.7. In addition to this non-standard arrow representation, conventional representations such as a symbolic expression, a graph and a table can be shown.

The above example shows that digital tools may integrate several of the four algebraic functionalities. For example, the graphing calculator was introduced as a graphing tool, but offers important features for probability and statistics as well. CAS software usually includes a programming language and comes with modules for geometry, graphing, tables and statistics. And, the other way around, the originally dynamic geometry software GeoGebra now includes a CAS module. In the meantime, distinguishing different algebraic functionalities may help to choose an appropriate digital tool, whether it is open and versatile or dedicated to specific educational purposes, and to be aware of one's priorities.

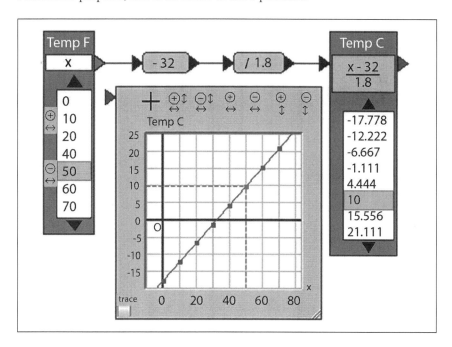

FIGURE 5.7 Visualization of a function as an operation chain with additional representations (www.dwo.nl/en).

5.2.2 Pedagogical Roles of Digital Tools for Algebra

In addition to the different algebraic functionalities that digital tools offer, they also may play different pedagogical roles, that is, different roles in algebra education. We distinguish the pedagogical roles of digital technology as a tool for doing algebra, as an environment to practice skills and as an environment for concept development (see Figure 5.8, based on Drijvers, Boon, & Van Reeuwijk, 2011). Let us briefly elaborate each of these roles.

The pedagogical function of tools for *doing algebra* comes down to outsourcing algebra to the tool, that acts as an "algebra assistant" who does part of the work for you, so that you yourself can concentrate on the core issues at stake. At first glance, this is a user's perspective rather than a learner's perspective. However, the student, while using the tool this way, has to decide on what and how to delegate to the device, and how to interpret the results and to critically consider them. As such, there is also a pedagogical aspect in this type of use.

As a straightforward example of using a tool for doing algebra, the left part of the screen in Figure 5.9 shows how a student may use the "expand" and "factor" commands in a CAS to rewrite a function formula. The interpretation of the results, however, is less evident. Only a skilled student may be able to "read through" the formulas, and recognize the zeros and the vertical asymptote of the graph in the second form, and the equation of the other asymptote in the third form. The center part of Figure 5.9 shows the graph of a function h defined by $h(x) = x^3 - 6x^2 + 9x + 1$, drawn by a CAS—also a matter of outsourcing. Inspecting the graph leads to the conjecture that it is symmetric in the point (2, 3). This can be checked by outsourcing the algebraic simplification to the CAS as well, which is done in the right part of Figure 5.9. The result, 3, shows that, indeed, the average function value of two points of equal horizontal distance to 2 equals 3. These examples emphasize how outsourcing algebraic activity requires algebraic insight!

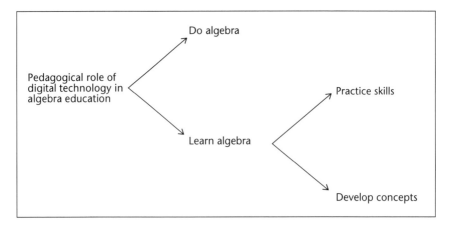

FIGURE 5.8 Three pedagogical roles of digital tools for algebra.

Algebra Education in the Digital Era **115**

The pedagogical role of *practicing skills* is in some countries used on a large scale in algebra education. Many online applets are available to practice skills such as equation solving, expansion and factorization. The advantages are that students can practice as long as they want, in private, and don't need a teacher. The tasks can be randomized and feedback can be offered. Still, research findings on the learning gains of these types of activities are not unanimous. In some cases, the online practice did not lead to better achievement (Drijvers, Doorman, Kirshner, Hoogveld, & Boon, 2014).

As an example of digitally supported practice, Figure 5.10 shows two screens—the task on the left, and a correct solution on the right—in which students are asked to reconstruct the steps in a solution of a linear equation by selecting the actions in the light colored boxes. Although the task here is somewhat original, and, therefore hopefully motivating to students, the goal essentially is to practice the stepwise solution of equations.

The use of digital tools for *developing concepts* is the most subtle application in algebra education. Digital tools can offer powerful images, connected representations and impressive dynamics. A seamless connection to previous knowledge and corresponding representations, making explicit the sometimes hidden algebraic messages in the work with the technology, or transferring the findings to the pen-and-paper environment, all this is not self-evident. To achieve this, teacher guidance and exchange with peers seem to be crucial.

As an example, Figure 5.11 shows a screen shot from the Algebra Applet that was also used in Figure 5.7. To study the behavior of three different functions (find intersection points and compare growth rates), the students collapsed the original

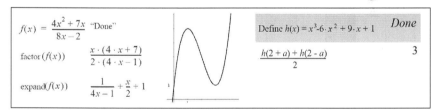

FIGURE 5.9 Outsource algebra to a CAS, in this case TI-Nspire.

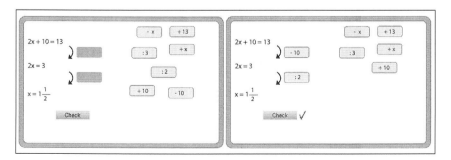

FIGURE 5.10 Identifying solution steps (http://ws.fisme.science.uu.nl/dwo/en/).

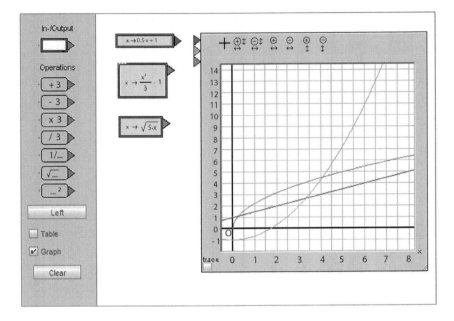

FIGURE 5.11 Functions as objects (http://ws.fisme.science.uu.nl/dwo/en/).

arrow chains, like the one in Figure 5.7, into more compact and more conventional function notations in the three boxes to the left of the graphs. This not only saves space on the screen and as such helps the student to keep an overview, but it also fosters an object view of each of the three functions, rather than the input–output process view that was dominant in the extended arrow chain representation (see Section 3.8). As such, this applet's built-in feature offers a means for deepening the students' conception of function.

Of course, the three pedagogical functions of ICT (as tool, exercise environment and environment for conceptual development) are not mutually exclusive. The first and the third function, in particular, can go together well. As an example of this, the Barbie Bungee activity (Zordak, 2008) presents students with the challenge of finding the best number of identical elastic bands to string together to make a bungee rope for a safe jump. This bungee rope is for dropping a toy doll from a large height (such as 4 meters) above a hard surface. Students experiment with small numbers of elastic bands (making short ropes) and small heights in the classroom and capture their data in a table (Figure 5.12). They then fit an algebraic model to the distance the toy drops as a function of the number of elastic bands. A linear function $y = mx + c$ is usually a good fit to the data collected. A nice way to do this is to graph the data (e.g., using a spreadsheet or graphics calculator) and then use the ICT's linear regression facility to obtain the equation and draw the line of best fit. For some students, fitting the line by eye can be adequate to achieve the purpose of the lesson. It is not necessary for students to understand the theory of regression lines—using the technology as a black box is quite appropriate.

Next, students use the line of best fit (graphical or algebraic) to make a prediction of the best number of elastic bands to use for the high bungee jump, and later they test it with their own toys. Students are very careful to predict when they use their own childhood toys! The learning objectives of this rich activity will, of course, vary according to the teaching context and what the teacher wishes to emphasize, but both theoretical algebra concepts and important principles of mathematical modeling can be taught and/or experienced. For example, students can discover that c is the height of the doll (gaining new appreciation for the meaning of the intercept of a graph and the constant term in a linear function). They may learn that m is the length of one stretched elastic band, which provides a specific example of how the slope of the graph and the coefficient m is a rate: in this case it converts the number of bands to centimeters. Variation in the data from the straight-line graph gives an important lesson about real world modeling. Because of its role in describing functional behavior, algebra is a powerful tool for modeling real world phenomena. An emphasis on modeling can, and should, contribute to two sets of goals—to teach algebra with meaning, and to learn to use algebra to model the real world. In this example, the role of ICT as an algebra assistant to which work can be outsourced—the first pedagogical role—applies to the use of the regression procedure as a black box. In the meantime, the results of this contribute to the students' insight into linear functions, and as such to their conceptual understanding, which relates to the third pedagogical role.

To summarize this section, we identified three possible pedagogical roles for digital tools in algebra education. Of course, this is not an exhaustive classification, and the above example shows that different roles may be combined; still, we do believe that such a global indication of the functions that digital tools may have in the teaching and learning of algebra may help teachers to decide on the ways they will or will not integrate specific tools into their teaching at particular moments.

Number of Rubber Bands (x)	Jump Distance in Centimeters (y)
2	
4	
6	
8	
10	
12	

FIGURE 5.12 Table to record data in the Barbie Bungee activity (adapted from http://illuminations.nctm.org/Lesson.aspx?id=2157).

5.3 Core Algebra Entities With Digital Means

In Section 5.2, we addressed the algebraic functionalities of digital tools and the pedagogical opportunities they offer, and illustrated this with examples. In the present section, we elaborate on these pedagogical opportunities, and focus on the teaching and learning of some of the core entities of algebra described in Subsection 1.2.3: variable, equation and function. In terms of the three pedagogical roles depicted in Figure 5.8, the main role digital tools play in this section is the third one, the environment for concept development.

5.3.1 Variable

The notion of variable is clearly central in school algebra. As indicated in Chapter 1, it is a multi-faceted concept with many different meanings and different roles (Freudenthal, 1983). As outlined in Chapter 3, variables, represented by the letters in algebraic expressions and formulas, should not be understood as abbreviated names for objects, but rather as standing for numbers, for example numbers of objects or quantities. The "fruit-salad" pedagogy was described as a didactical approach that will not reduce this confusion. In Chapter 1, the following facets of the concept of variable are described: placeholder, unknown, varying quantity, generalized number and parameter. We will now revisit each of these facets, and show how the variable representations within digital tools implicitly or explicitly prioritize them and may contribute to fostering an understanding of variable.

The first and probably most straightforward notion of variable is the *placeholder* for a numerical value. Figure 5.13 shows an example of this facet: in the first line, the value 2 is stored in a placeholder called A. In the third line, this numerical value is retrieved and substituted in the expression. A cell in a spreadsheet similarly reflects a placeholder view on variable. If one fills cell A1 with a numerical value, and then enters the formula A1^2 in cell B1, A1 acts as a placeholder for the value stored there.

```
2→A
                    2
(A+3)²*5
                  125
```

FIGURE 5.13   Variable as placeholder on a calculator.

A second facet of the notion of variable is the *unknown* number. This view is very present when solving equations. As for the role of digital tools in solving equations and dealing with unknowns we refer to Subsection 5.3.2.

The third facet of the notion of variable concerns the *varying quantity* or *changing number*. In Subsection 5.2.2, the Barbie Bungee activity provided an example of the variable (e.g. height) really varying. As a second example, Figure 5.14 shows a window in the Algebra Arrows applet, as was the case in Figures 5.7 and 5.11. This time, however, the student drags the grey point on the bottom trace bar to investigate the graph of the function f with $f(x) = \sqrt{x^2 + 3}$, and in particular to investigate if the function values approach x when x increases. This technique of tracing reflects the changing number face of variable. Clearly, this view often appears in the context of function, which will be addressed further in Subsection 5.3.3.

When the variable acts as a *generalized number*, it is used to describe general properties. This view of variable is manifest while simplifying or rewriting algebraic expressions with a computer algebra tool. For example, in lines 2, 4 and 5 of Figure 5.4, which show CAS procedures to rewrite expressions, the variables p, q, a and b symbolize generalized numbers, as the simplifications hold in general, i.e., for all numerical values substituted for them.

The *parameter*, finally, is a higher order variable in the sense that its value determines the situation as a whole. For example, consider Figure 5.5 and assume that the values of b, c and d are fixed. The value of the parameter a, then, determines the formula and the graph of function f. If a has a fixed value too, it acts as a

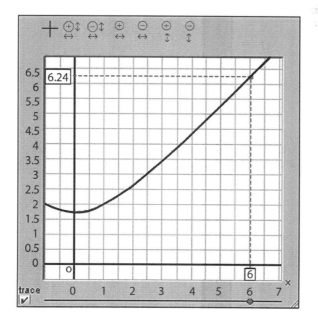

FIGURE 5.14 Variable as changing number while tracing a function.

placeholder parameter. Only then can the functions *f* and *g* be graphed. If we want to know for which value of *a* the graph of *f* passes through the point (–2, –2), the parameter *a* becomes an unknown. A CAS command such as solve (*f* (–2) = 2, *a*) will find this unknown (incorporating the value of the known *b*). If we want to prove that for all values of *a* the point (0, 3) is on the graph, *a* is a generalized number. In this case, a CAS command to test whether *f* (0) = 3 should return the value "true." And, finally, if we want to investigate the effect of the value of *a* on the graphs of *f* and *h* through dragging its value with the slider bar, *a* gets the character of a changing number. Again, the type of technique used in the digital environment corresponds to different faces of the notion of variable.

To conclude this section, we once more observe that the notion of variable has different conceptual facets. These facets are reflected in the ways in which variables are represented and used in digital environments, in combination, of course, with the task being tackled. As there is an interplay between techniques that students apply while using a digital tool and their conceptual understanding, a careful match of these techniques and understandings is a prerequisite of effective technology-rich algebra teaching. As a consequence, the choice of the tasks, the digital tool and the techniques to use it should reflect the pedagogical intentions addressed in the teaching: the storage of values as shown in Figure 5.13 fits better if the goal is to foster a placeholder view, while tracing the graph (Figure 5.14) highlights (and may evoke!) the changing number view on variable.

5.3.2 Equation and Equivalence

As described in Chapter 1, equation is another core entity in initial algebra. Solving an equation comes down to finding all possible values of a variable, in its role of an unknown number, that make an algebraic relation true. In Section 3.7, it is explained that in equations of the type <expression> = <constant>, where the left-hand side in some cases may be seen in terms of a chain of operations starting with the unknown, one can solve the equation by undoing these operations one by one (or by guessing a number and adjusting through proportion like the Egyptian method in Section 2.2). The targeted constant of this reverse strategy can be used as a starting value. Figure 5.15 shows such a strategy in an applet environment for the equation $3(x + 4) + 2 = 29$. The upper arrow chain represents the equation's left-hand side, with its intermediate forms. The bottom part represents the "undoing" strategy with the outcome of 29 as a point of departure. Clearly, the solution of the equation is 5, and the digital tool supports the reverse strategy that was already described in Section 3.7.

This type of equation of the form <expression> = <constant>, with the unknown appearing only once, may also be solved using the so-called cover-up strategy. As is shown in Figure 4.10, this strategy comes down to covering an expression within the equation to solve, to finding the value of this expression in order to make the equation true, and to writing down a (hopefully easier) equation that follows from this. In terms of the process–object duality mentioned in Section

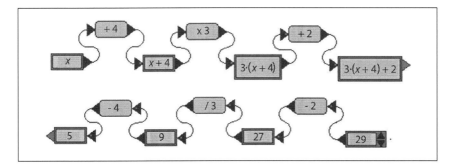

FIGURE 5.15 Solving an equation using the reverse "unpacking" strategy with the applet Algebra Arrows (http://ws.fisme.science.uu.nl/dwo/en/).

3.3, this strategy requires an object view of the expressions to be covered; also, some insight into the structure of the equation as a whole is needed, which may be seen as part of students' symbol sense (Arcavi, 1994). Making the arrow diagrams of Figure 5.15 or Figure 3.9 builds insight into the links between an algebraic expression and the operations that produce it (and their order).

The limitation of these two quite similar strategies, however, is that they only apply to a specific class of equations. A more general approach is the balance strategy, also addressed in Section 3.7. Dedicated digital tools are available to support the development of this strategy while offering feedback in different degrees of sophistication. Once the "do the same to both sides" principle is understood, this balance strategy can also be applied in more general tools such as CAS. Figure 5.16 shows an example, in which the first step, the expansion, is done by the software by default (called "autosimplification"). Next, the student identifies the relevant steps to make: add 4 to both sides, subtract $6x$ from both sides and divide both sides by -2. Note the specialized CAS notation for operating on both sides of an equation signified by the brackets around the whole equation. The point here is that the algebraic manipulations are outsourced to the CAS (cf. Figure 5.9), but with a pedagogical goal to make students focus on the strategic decisions on which operation to carry out next, as is the case in the example in Figure 5.10. In terms of the processes and objects mentioned in Sections 3.3 and Subsection 3.7.1, this technique of CAS use both requires and helps to develop an object view on equation, as the equation is subject to the operation of adding $6x$ to both sides, for example. A productive lesson can be based around students solving equations such as that in Figure 5.16 in a specified number of steps. The example shows solving in three steps. As a kind of game, students can be asked if this equation can be solved in exactly 4, 7, 11 or 2 non-trivial steps. This activity separates two aspects of equation solving—the question of what moves are legal because they retain the integrity of the solution set, and the different question of what moves make for easy solving in a pen-and-paper environment. As an aside, it should be noted that the autosimplification aspects of CAS make it impossible to demonstrate some legal

$$4(x - 1) = 3*(2x + 1)$$
$$\rightarrow 4x - 4 = 6x + 3$$

$$(4x - 4 = 6x + 3) + 4$$
$$\rightarrow 4x = 6x + 7$$

$$(4x = 6x + 7) - 6x$$
$$\rightarrow -2x = 7$$

$$(-2x = 7) / (-2)$$
$$\rightarrow x = -\frac{7}{2}$$

FIGURE 5.16 Solving an equation using the balance strategy in the GeoGebra CAS (Drijvers & Barzel, 2012).

equation solving moves with the open tool. For example, GeoGebra will not support solving $4(x - 1) = 3(2x + 1)$ by first dividing by 4, because it immediately autosimplifies the entered equation to $4x - 4 = 6x + 3$. Special applets which are designed for teaching the balance method can be more useful (Drijvers & Barzel, 2012). An example is the applet Algebra Balance Scales from the National Library of Virtual Manipulatives (n.d.).

A different approach to equation solving is a graphical one: solving an equation can be seen as finding intersection points of graphs. Now that graphing tools are so widely available, in particular in the form of graphing calculators and software, this is a very effective method. As there is no algebraic manipulation involved, it has the advantage of being applicable to equations beyond the few special algebraic structures for which we have routine solving methods. Also, it contributes to an intuitive understanding of equation in a graphical way. For example, the equation $x^7 - 7x^5 + 5x^3 - 3x = x + 1$ can be solved through an approximation of the intersection point of the graphs of functions f and g with $f(x) = x^7 - 7x^5 + 5x^3 - 3x$ and $g(x) = x + 1$ in the left part of Figure 5.17. However, the right part of the same figure shows that zooming out reveals more intersection points, so more solutions

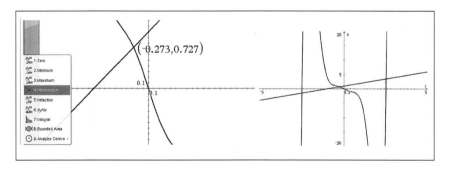

FIGURE 5.17 Solving an equation using an intersect procedure on a graphing calculator.

to the equation. To apply this method, therefore, students need to understand that the left-hand side and the right-hand side of an equation both can be seen as functions of the variables involved, so that the first co-ordinates of the intersection points of the corresponding graphs represent the solutions of the equation. Also, they should take care that the viewing window is such that all intersection points are visible in order to be sure that all solutions are found.

Of course, if a CAS is available, solving equations can be completely outsourced. However, this is not as straightforward to students as it may seem. For example, it was found that for equations of the form <expression> = 0, students sometimes forget to add the "= 0" (which by the way is accepted by some CASs) and seem to confuse expressions and equations (Drijvers, 2003; Drijvers, Godino, Font, & Trouche, 2013). Also, it may be difficult for them to indicate the correct unknown at the end of the solve command. It can be a surprise to see, in lines 1 and 2 of Figure 5.18, that solving with respect to a leads to a different result, compared to the usual solving with respect to x. To deal with solutions that are expressions rather than numerical values also challenges students' understanding of equation and demands an object view on expressions. Finally, the last two lines of Figure 5.18 show that not all equations can be solved exactly (both in theory and also depending on the power of the individual CAS). The example shows how the CAS may just return the equation if an exact answer has been requested or provide one or more numerical answers (real or complex), depending on the settings.

Related to equations is the notion of equivalence. In fact, equivalence can be understood by students in different ways (Kieran & Drijvers, 2006). The first way reflects the definition provided in Subsection 1.2.3: two expressions are equivalent if the domains of substitution are identical for both, and all numbers allowed for substitution in the first expression yield the same result in the second, and vice versa. This can be verified by transforming one expression into the other by means of legitimate algebraic operations, which is the second view. While doing so, however, the domain has to be taken into account and this is where the use of digital tools may become sophisticated. For example, the table of function values in Figure 5.19 provided by the Excel spreadsheet software may suggest the

solve($a \cdot x^2 + b \cdot x + c = 0, x$)	$x = \dfrac{\sqrt{b^2 - 4 \cdot a \cdot c} - b}{2 \cdot a}$ or $x = -\dfrac{\left(\sqrt{b^2 - 4 \cdot a \cdot c} - b\right)}{2 \cdot a}$
solve($a \cdot x^2 + b \cdot x + c = 0, a$)	$a = \dfrac{-(b \cdot x + c)}{x^2}$
solve($x^7 - x = 6, x$)	$x \cdot (x^6 - 1) = 6$
solve($x^7 - x = 6, x$)	$x = 1.32917$

FIGURE 5.18 Solving equations using CAS (from Drijvers, Godino, Font, & Trouche, 2013).

x	1	2	3	4	5	6	7	8	9	(x^2 − 100)/(x + 10) → **x − 10**
x − 10	−9	−8	−7	−6	−5	−4	−3	−2	−1	
(x^2 − 100)/(x +10)	−9	−8	−7	−6	−5	−4	−3	−2	−1	

FIGURE 5.19 Table of values made in a spreadsheet (left), and symbolic simplification using the GeoGebra CAS (right).

equivalence of the two expressions. The use of the computer algebra module in GeoGebra to simplify one expression into the other supports this conjecture. However, the two do not have the same domain: the first expression is defined for $x = -10$, but the second one isn't. Therefore, some care is required: while simplifying, computer algebra software may take a tolerant stance towards domain restrictions while simplifying expressions without attending to domain constraints (see Figure 5.4), and would simplify $\frac{x^2 - 100}{x + 10}$ as $x - 10$, sometimes with a message to exclude the case that $x = -10$.

To summarize this section, we see that there are different ways to view equations and equivalence, each with different strategies to deal with them. Different digital tools, and the different techniques available for use, may foster or discourage some of these views. As was the case in the previous section, the choice of a digital tool therefore impacts on the learning process and should reflect the teacher's pedagogical intentions.

5.3.3 Function

In Section 3.8 a function is described as a mathematical object with different aspects and interpretations, such as instructions for processing numbers, an input–output machine, a dependency relationship in which changes of the independent variable cause determined changes in the dependent one, and an entity with different representations and properties, which may be subject to higher order processes such as differentiation. As was the case for the notions of variable, equations and equivalence, different digital tools highlight these different aspects of the function concept in different ways (Doorman et al., 2012). Let us consider some examples focusing on functions of one real variable.

- The function as an input–output machine or rule: The arrow chains in Figures 5.7 and 5.15 typically provide an input–output view of function. Even though not all functions can be represented as operation chains and these representations are not common in higher mathematics, these "function machines" symbolize the input–output process in an accessible way. We believe that it is beneficial to explore chains of operations like these in the phase of introducing the notion of function, as it is an intuitive notion of processing input into output.

Clearly, digital tools that provide these operation chain representations stress a view of function as a calculation process rather than as a mathematical object.
- The function as a dependency relationship: To investigate the effect that changing the independent variable has on the dependent function value using digital tools, students could start to systematically change the input value in operation chains that represent the function. However, this is a time-consuming approach. An easier way to achieve this is to browse through the table of function values that, for example, can be generated by a spreadsheet (see Figure 5.6) or by a graphing calculator. A more continuous way to investigate the change of the dependent variable is by tracing a graph of the function, as is shown in Figure 5.14. Most function graphing tools provide some kind of trace option, and this allows a feeling for the functional relationship. Investigations of this type no longer stress the local point-to-point relationship that is so present in the operation chain representation, but rather allow the student to re-consider the function, through its graph, as a whole. As such this might contribute to the development of an object view of function.
- The function as an object with different representations and properties: Functions can be seen as mathematical objects that can be classified according to specific properties or characteristics. For example, linear functions have straight lines as graphs, and trigonometric functions provide "wave-like" graphs. Such "function-objects" can be manipulated through digital means and multiple representations become accessible through them. In the example shown in Figure 5.5, two linear functions can be manipulated as a whole by changing parameter values such as slope or intercept through slider bars. The two functions also form the building blocks for their product, which has a parabola as its graph. Also, we can use digital tools such as CASs to define functions and give them a name, so as to ease later work. This naming action stresses the function as a mathematical object.

One of the difficulties with the notion of function is that a function has different, but interrelated, representations. In addition to a verbal description, a function can be represented through a formula, through a table of values and through a graph and possibly an operation chain. These different representations are linked. Many phenomena in one representation have counterparts in the others. For example, an x-intercept corresponds to a root of the function. On the other hand, some features or properties may appear clearly in one representation and remain obscure in another. A root of the function formula, for example, is clear in the graph and in a table of values, but not clear in the formula itself or an operation chain. An important opportunity offered by technology is that it can juxtapose multiple representations, so that the relationships between them can be investigated. In the literature, this opportunity to use multiple representations, dynamically linked, has been considered as one of the main affordances of digital tools for mathematics education. Figure 5.7, for example, integrates an arrow chain representation with a formula, a table and a graph. In the software a change in one representation can be automatically reflected in another. In Figure 5.11, the graphs and formulas of three functions are provided, which supports reflection on how the differences between the three formulas impact on the three graphs.

Indeed, representing formulas and graphs is a powerful affordance of many digital tools for mathematics. Figure 5.20 shows a sheaf of graphs of the function f, each one corresponding to a particular value of the parameter b in $f(x) = x^4 + b \cdot x^2 + 1$. Imagine that we connect the minima, and so we get another curve. It might be a parabola, but can we prove this is really the case?

To answer this question, we switch from the graphical representation to the symbolic one: at the minima, the derivative with respect to x equals 0. This means:

$$4x^3 + 2bx = 0$$

Students are used to solving equations with respect to x. However, in this case it is easier to let the parameter play the role of the unknown and to solve with respect to b:

$$b = -2x^2$$

Substituting this expression for b into the function formula yields:

$$y = x^4 - 2x^2 \cdot x^2 + 1 = 1 - x^4$$

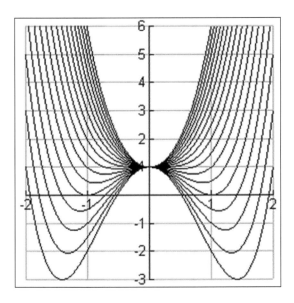

FIGURE 5.20 What kind of curve passes through the minima? (Adapted from Drijvers, Boon, & Van Reeuwijk, 2011).

Thus the curve through the minima is of degree 4, and although it looks like a parabola, it is not one!

As we see in this example, working on the symbolic representations may help to understand the graphical ones. And the other way around, graphs may help us to identify algebraic properties. This exemplifies the opportunity that digital tools may offer to re-sequence the curriculum and to re-order the topics and their representations in a teaching sequence (Heid, 1988). For example, the pathway from graphs to algebra is made possible by graphing tools that allow for high-speed accurate access to graphs with which students might not yet be familiar. With high-speed zooming and easily modified viewing windows, students can explore these new functions.

Overall, this section shows that the different aspects of the concept of functions of one real variable have their counterparts in different digital tools, or in different ways to use them. Again, this shows that the choice of the digital tool and the technique to use it may impact on students' conceptual development and therefore should match with the teacher's pedagogical intentions. In particular, the use of multiple linked representations is one of the strong affordances of digital tools for algebra.

5.4 Teaching and Learning Algebra With Digital Means

The previous section suggests that the use of digital tools may help to foster the understanding of key concepts in algebra such as variable, equation and function. We have seen some promising examples and nothing seems to hinder a large-scale implementation of technology-intensive algebra education. But are things as straightforward as that? In this section, we take a more reflective and research-oriented perspective, while zooming out on the examples and considering the hard question of what may work and what may not in algebra teaching with digital tools.

What can we learn from research studies on ICT in algebra education? The overall findings from review studies, that synthesize results from many other studies, is that students who used digital tools in their algebra courses did better than those who didn't: the use of digital tools in algebra education has a positive but modest effect (e.g., see Rakes, Valentine, McGatha, & Ronau, 2010). To phrase this in more technical terms, the effect sizes in experimental studies are small, but positive and statistically significant. This suggests that ICT in algebra education "works." But in the meantime, we can be disappointed by the limited size of the effects. Why aren't benefits larger? Why are there studies that show no effect? What are possible hindrances? What are decisive factors in making ICT work or not?

The answer to this is that the use of digital tools in algebra education is a subtle matter that should be treated carefully in two ways: first by offering appropriate tasks with appropriate tools, and second by treating these tasks in fruitful ways while teaching. We now elaborate on each of these two points.

What is essential in offering appropriate tasks with appropriate tools is that the ways in which the tools are used corresponds to the targeted conceptual understanding. For example, if the teaching goal is to make students aware of the tree structure of an expression, and the order of operations within it, a digital tool such as Algebra Trees represents this better than an environment that requires the input of expressions in sequential line entry format like sqrt(a^2+b^2) (see Figure 5.21).

As a second example, we once more refer to the cover-up strategy for solving equations. As is shown in Figure 4.10, each of the two conceptual aspects of this strategy is reflected in a technique to use the applet. The first aspect is noticing the equation's structure and finding a sub-expression to cover. This comes down to symbol sense (Arcavi, 1994) and is reflected in the applet's technique of moving the mouse to highlight the sub-expression in question. The second aspect is

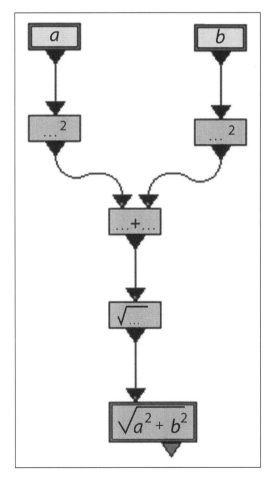

FIGURE 5.21 Tree representation in Algebra Trees (www.fisme.science.uu.nl/toepassingen/17003/).

concerned with finding the value of the selected sub-expression. This is called global substitution (Wenger, 1987). This corresponds to entering the value in the applet, which is automatically checked. So the two mental processes match the two techniques available in the applet and this may explain the success of students using the applet (Jupri, Drijvers, & Van den Heuvel-Panhuizen, 2015). Also, the techniques embedded in the applet have their counterparts in pen-and-paper: covering a sub-expression can be done by putting an oval around it, and assigning a value is similar on paper and on a screen. This match between techniques to use the tool and to use pen-and-paper is a strong point, with the applet providing the additional features of ease of use and immediate feedback.

What holds for dedicated tools, such as the ones in the two examples above, is particularly true for more open and general mathematical tools such as CASs. A third example of the interplay between ways of using the digital tool and algebraic thinking concerns solving a parametric quadratic equation using a computer algebra CAS calculator. Even if one might think that using the CAS solve command makes this trivial, Grade 9 students encountered difficulties that reflect both technical and conceptual obstacles (Drijvers, Godino, Font, & Trouche, 2013). For example, many of them forgot to specify the unknown x, which is understandable, as the choice of the unknown usually remains implicit in pen-and-paper equation solving (especially when it is x). Also, while copying the result from the calculator screen into their notebooks, many students were not able to write down the square root part correctly because they did not copy the scope of the square root sign carefully (see Figure 5.22). Of course, these initial issues can be overcome while teaching, but they do show the non-trivial technical and conceptual aspects of using CAS.

The above examples illustrate the interplay between techniques to use the digital tool on the one hand and algebraic insight on the other. If there is a good match between the two, they will develop simultaneously: technical mastery and insight will co-emerge (Kieran & Drijvers, 2006). In research on the use of digital tools in mathematics education, this process is called instrumental genesis: the

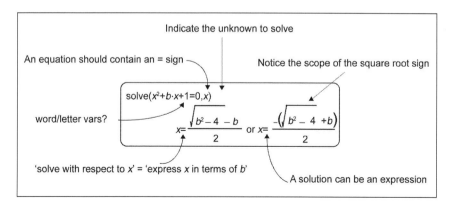

FIGURE 5.22 Student difficulties in solving a quadratic equation using computer algebra (Drijvers, Godino, Font, & Trouche, 2013).

digital tool becomes a meaningful instrument in the hands of the student (Artigue, 2002). In short, the techniques needed to use the tool for the task should invite the development of the algebraic insight targeted in the teaching.

Now what does the phrase used above, "treating these tasks in fruitful ways while teaching," mean? If we want to use digital tools so that students simultaneously develop the technical skills needed and the algebraic insight involved, the teacher cannot just step back and leave the job to the digital environment. Rather, students need guidance, support and explanations during this process since they will not always be aware of the intertwinement of technique and insight. The teacher will need to act as a conductor who organizes the teaching in such a way, that the "mathematics hidden in the work with the tool" becomes explicit and subject to discussion. As such, the use of digital tools is not making the teacher superfluous; the teacher remains a crucial guide in the students' learning processes albeit with a redefined role.

It is here that the metaphor of orchestration comes in: the teacher has a role in orchestrating the learning process through designing settings that optimize the learning with the digital tools. As an example, Trouche (2004) describes the so-called Sherpa orchestration, in which one student, the "Sherpa-student," uses the technology in front of the class, guided by the teacher. Delegating some teacher roles to students can advance the learning of all students. Other examples of orchestrations are provided by Drijvers, Doorman, Boon, Reed, and Gravemeijer (2010) and Drijvers, Tacoma, Besamusca, Doorman, and Boon (2013). As we discussed in Chapter 4, such teaching with digital tools may require a thorough re-learning process by teachers.

As a conclusion to this section, algebra learning may benefit from the use of both dedicated educational digital tools and open mathematical tools. Decisive for this benefit is the match between the targeted algebraic insights and methods, the techniques to use the digital tool and the conventional pen-and-paper techniques. If orchestrated well by the teacher, the use of the digital tool will foster the co-emergence of insight, skill and tool mastery, as well as developing a sense of purpose for the students.

5.5 Chapter Summary

In this chapter we considered the impact of digital technology on teaching and learning practices in algebra education, including their opportunities and constraints. We now review the chapter's key points. The core question is how digital technology is changing algebra education, including both its curricular content goals and its teaching and learning practices. The main message is that while teaching algebra, we have to carefully consider what each of the different tools has to offer in the light of specific learning goals in the field of algebra, and how this potential can be exploited in a fruitful way.

To investigate the impact of digital technology on teaching and learning practices in algebra, we set up a global inventory of the algebraic functionality of these tools in Section 5.2, with four main categories: symbolic functionality, graphing functionality, table functionality, and visualization and representation functionality. These functionalities may also be available during tests and examinations, as in some countries the use of computer algebra during assessment is allowed. As for the pedagogical roles, we distinguished the roles of a tool for doing algebra, a tool for practicing skills and a tool for developing concepts. In none of the three roles does digital technology offer a panacea for the intrinsic difficulties of algebra education; they do have a potential contribution.

In Section 5.3, we addressed the different kinds of opportunities these digital tools offer to the teaching and learning of core algebra concepts: variable, equation and function. The examples show some new and promising approaches to these concepts that may foster students' insights and skills. In the meantime, we notice that the effect of such tools will largely depend on the timing, the pedagogical context, the task and the type of students. In case of a mismatch between tool use and algebraic purpose, the benefit of using ICT might get lost.

This brought us to the reflection on the teaching and learning of algebra in Section 5.4. It was shown that digital tools for algebra support different sets of representations of algebraic concepts and invite different techniques, which emphasize specific insights into algebraic concepts. The match between these techniques and insights is an important factor in a successful implementation of technology in algebra education. The development of the emerging techniques for using the tool and the corresponding algebraic understanding, called instrumental genesis, is a subtle process that has to be carefully orchestrated by the teacher. The benefit of using digital tools for algebra largely depends on the success of this instrumental genesis and orchestration.

In the introduction, we briefly addressed the impact of digital tools on the curricular goals of school algebra. In retrospect, we have highlighted some opportunities for technology-based curricula with different types of goals and problems. What we observe in algebra education, however, is an evolution rather than a revolution. Complex procedures will rarely be carried out with pen-and-paper in practice, with so many sophisticated digital tools all around. Therefore, a gradual shift may take place from a mainly procedural curriculum towards a more insight-oriented curriculum, in which the procedural work, after an initial experience of the technical aspects of algebra, may be sometimes outsourced to technology. For example, advanced algebraic simplification and techniques to find anti-derivatives are gradually disappearing from final tests in many countries and are now outsourced to CAS tools, just as four-digit multiplications are no longer practiced too often because we have four-function calculators. More stress in the curricula on different ways of thinking about problems, on problem solving strategies, and on symbol sense, seems appropriate. Even if we consider pen-and-paper work as one of the means to acquire a sense of symbolic manipulation, digital tools may offer means to use real data, to bring the real world into the classroom (see the Barbie Bungee example in Subsection 5.2.2), to explore regularity and

5.6 Thinking Further

Section 5.2 Digital Tools for Algebra

1. In Subsection 5.2, different algebraic functionalities of digital tools for mathematics are distinguished, as well as three different pedagogical roles.
Activity: find an example of a digital task using a digital tool and decide on its algebraic functionality and its pedagogical role. Discuss the possible advantages and disadvantages of using the digital tool with your colleagues. Hint: you can use the hyperlinks provided in the figures of this chapter as a source of inspiration.

Section 5.3 Core Algebra Entities With Digital Means

2. In Section 5.3.1, it is outlined how different technological tools may prioritize specific facets of the notion of variable.
Activity: consider the lens formula $\frac{1}{f} = \frac{1}{v} + \frac{1}{b}$ (see Section 4.5). Which facet of the variable b is at stake if …
   - one uses a graphing tool to investigate how v changes if b gets bigger, with f remaining constant?
   - one uses CAS to find the value of b when $f = \frac{6}{5}$ and $v = \frac{1}{2}$?
   - one uses CAS to rewrite the formula as $f = \ldots$?
   - one uses a slider bar in a dynamic geometry system to investigate the influence of a changing value of b on the graph of f as a function of v?
3. The use of digital technology for algebra may open horizons for generalization. For example, if we look back at the example presented in Figure 5.20 in Section 5.3, one might wonder if there is a family of functions for which the curve through the minima indeed is a parabola.
Activity: consider the family of functions with $f(x) = x^2 + b \cdot x + 1$ for different values of the parameter b and a fixed value of n. Find the equation of the curve through the minima and prove that it is a parabola only when the original curves are parabolas as well.
4. As indicated in Subsection 5.3.2, CAS may simplify expressions without paying attention to domain restrictions.
Activity: use a computer algebra tool to investigate if seemingly equivalent forms share the same domain. Next, read the part on equivalence in the Kieran and Drijvers (2006) paper.

Section 5.4 Teaching and Learning Algebra With Digital Means

5. Section 5.4 suggests relating the techniques with the digital tool with the textbook content and with the conventional pen-and-paper work.
   Activity: prepare a whole-class discussion to synthesize the students' work. Make sure you can show their digital work and also have a white board available on which you can write the algebraic work by hand. Compare differences and similarities in using the two media with your students and discuss the results with your colleagues.
6. In Section 5.4, it is stressed that students develop appropriate techniques for using a tool, for example, by showing important elements in a short demonstration at the start of an activity.
   Activity: prepare a 5-minute demonstration to show the main technical aspects of building a table of function values using a spreadsheet (or for another situation), and discuss what students may learn from such a presentation.
7. In Section 5.4, an interesting working format, the so-called Sherpa orchestration, is described. It includes having students use the technological device in front of the class. This will help technical skills to converge and it offers valuable feedback on the learning process to you as a teacher.
   Activity: read Trouche's (2004) paper on the Sherpa student arrangement and, if possible, try it out in your classroom. Discuss the experience with your colleagues.
8. It is advisable to be explicit to students about the targeted outcomes, learning processes and style of working in ICT-rich activity.
   Activity: while preparing a technology-rich lesson in algebra, write down the way in which you will introduce the activity to the students with respect to what you expect from them (e.g., write down results, just explore, prove, use pen-and-paper algebra, ...). Try the lesson and compare and contrast your plan with the actual experience.
9. After students' hands-on work with technology, a whole-class discussion of the findings can be fruitful.
   Activity: prepare such a whole-class discussion in a concrete situation and think beforehand on the main points that you would want to come up. Consider how you will deal with the "explosion of methods"—when students can do a standard algebra task in many more ways than before.
10. Figure 5.22 shows some obstacles students may encounter while using computer algebra. It is important to have a feeling for the type of difficulties students may experience while using technology.
    Activity: carefully watch a student who starts to work in a new digital environment and notice all obstacles that hinder the targeted algebraic work and thinking. Read the article "Obstacles are opportunities" (Drijvers, 2002) and compare and contrast your experience with what is described in the paper.

11. During a technology-rich student activity, it may be a good teaching strategy to invite students to collaborate.
Activity: experiment with different forms of student collaboration during your technology-rich lessons, for example, students working in pairs, working in groups of three or four, appointing different roles (one using the device, another reporting the process, a third capturing the results …). Describe different ways of collaboration and explore more fully those that yield unexpected learning opportunities.

5.7 References

Arcavi, A. (1994). Symbol sense: Informal sense-making in formal mathematics. *For the Learning of Mathematics, 14*(3), 24–35. http://flm-journal.org/Articles/BFBFB3A8A2A03CF606513A05A22B.pdf (Accessed September 7, 2015).

Arcavi, A., & Hadas, N. (2000). Computer mediated learning: An example of an approach. *International Journal of Computers for Mathematical Learning, 5*(1), 25–45.

Artigue, M. (2002). Learning mathematics in a CAS environment: The genesis of a reflection about instrumentation and the dialectics between technical and conceptual work. *International Journal of Computers for Mathematical Learning, 7*, 245–274.

Doorman, M., Drijvers, P., Gravemeijer, K., Boon, P., & Reed, H. (2012). Tool use and the development of the function concept: From repeated calculations to functional thinking. *International Journal of Science and Mathematics Education, 10*(6).

Drijvers, P. (2002). Learning mathematics in a computer algebra environment: Obstacles are opportunities. *Zentralblatt für Didaktik der Mathematik, 34*(5), 221–228.

Drijvers, P. (2003). *Learning Algebra in a Computer Algebra Environment. Design Research on the Understanding of the Concept of Parameter.* Dissertation. Utrecht, the Netherlands: CD-Bèta press.

Drijvers, P., & Barzel, B. (2012). Equations with technology: Different tools, different views. *Mathematics Teaching, 228*, 14–19.

Drijvers, P., Boon, P., & Van Reeuwijk, M. (2011). Algebra and technology. In P. Drijvers (Ed.), *Secondary Algebra Education. Revisiting Topics and Themes and Exploring the Unknown* (pp. 179–202). Rotterdam: Sense.

Drijvers, P., Doorman, M., Boon, P., Reed, H., & Gravemeijer, K. (2010). The teacher and the tool: Instrumental orchestrations in the technology-rich mathematics classroom. *Educational Studies in Mathematics, 75*(2).

Drijvers, P., Doorman, M., Kirschner, P., Hoogveld, B., & Boon, P. (2014). The effect of online tasks for algebra on student achievement in grade 8. *Technology, Knowledge and Learning, 19*, 1–18.

Drijvers, P., Godino, J. D., Font, V., & Trouche, L. (2013). One episode, two lenses; a reflective analysis of student learning with computer algebra from instrumental and onto-semiotic perspectives. *Educational Studies in Mathematics, 82*(1), 23–49.

Drijvers, P., Tacoma, S., Besamusca, A., Doorman, M., & Boon, P. (2013). Digital resources inviting changes in mid-adopting teachers' practices and orchestrations. *ZDM Mathematics Education, 45*(7), 987–1001.

Dugdale, S. (1993). Functions and graphs – Perspectives on student thinking. In T. A. Romberg, E. Fennema, & T. P. Carpenter (Eds.), *Integrating Research on the Graphical Representations of Functions* (pp. 101–130). Hillsdale, NJ: Lawrence Erlbaum Associates Publishers.

Freudenthal, H. (1983). *Didactical Phenomenology of Mathematical Structures*. Dordrecht, the Netherlands: Reidel. www.gpdmatematica.org.ar/publicaciones/Freudenthal_Didactical_Phenomenology_of_Mathematical_Structures1983.pdf (accessed September 7, 2015).

Heid, M. K. (1988). Resequencing skills and concepts in applied calculus using the computer as a tool. *Journal for Research in Mathematics Education, 19*, 3–25.

Jupri, A., Drijvers, P., & Van den Heuvel-Panhuizen, M. (2015). *Digital Experience in Mathematics Education*. DOI: 10.1007/s40751-015-0004-2.

Kieran, C., & Drijvers, P. (2006). The co-emergence of machine techniques, paper-and-pencil techniques, and theoretical reflection: A study of CAS use in secondary school algebra. *International Journal of Computers for Mathematical Learning, 11*(2), 205–263.

National Council of Teachers of Mathematics (2008). *Technology in Teaching and Learning Mathematics. A Position of the National Council of Teachers of Mathematics*. www.nctm.org/Standards-and-Positions/Position-Statements/Technology-in-Teaching-and-Learning-Mathematics/ (accessed September 6, 2015).

National Library of Virtual Manipulatives (n.d.). *Algebra Balance Scales*. http://nlvm.usu.edu/en/nav/frames_asid_201_g_3_t_2.html?open=instructions&from=category_g_3_t_2.html (accessed September 6, 2015).

Rakes, C. R., Valentine, J. C., McGatha, M. B., & Ronau, R. N. (2010). Methods of instructional improvement in algebra: A systematic review and meta-analysis. *Review of Educational Research, 80*(3), 372–400.

Ruthven, K. (1990). The influence of graphic calculator use on translation from graphic to symbolic forms. *Educational Studies in Mathematics, 21*(5), 431–450.

Sangwin, C. (2013). *Computer Aided Assessment of Mathematics*. Oxford: Oxford University Press.

Trouche, L. (2004). Managing complexity of human/machine interactions in computerized learning environments: Guiding students' command process through instrumental orchestrations. *International Journal of Computers for Mathematical Learning, 9*, 281–307.

Wenger, R. H. (1987). Cognitive science and algebra learning. In A. Schoenfeld (Ed.), *Cognitive Science and Mathematical Education* (pp. 115–135). Hillsdale, NJ: Lawrence Erlbaum Associates.

Yerushalmy, M. & Swidan, O. (2012). Signifying the accumulation graph in a dynamic and multi-representation environment. *Educational Studies of Mathematics, 80*(3), 287–306.

Zordak, S. E. (2008). *Barbie Bungee*. Reston, VA: National Council of Teachers of Mathematics. http://illuminations.nctm.org/Lesson.aspx?id=2157 (accessed September 7, 2015).

EPILOGUE

In the last 50 years or so, mathematics education has become a full-fledged discipline of academic inquiry. This inquiry includes the systematic study of the design of instructional materials and research on learning and teaching. Thus, algebra, as a central topic in any high school mathematics curriculum around the world, was and still is under intensive scrutiny by teachers, teacher educators, curriculum developers and researchers. Countless journal articles, chapters and entire books were and still are devoted to algebra education, focusing on curricular approaches, student difficulties, teacher challenges and technological promises. Many questions and teaching dilemmas are still open, and rapid sociological and technological changes continue to impose a shifting educational agenda. The growth in mass secondary education and an appreciation of the importance of mathematics to economic innovation leads to widening the groups of students who are expected to learn algebra and technological change provides opportunities for new ways of doing algebra. Nevertheless, most of the existing body of accumulated knowledge serves (and will also serve in the future) as the basis upon which to reflect on algebra instruction and to propose and undertake adequate guidelines for action. In this book, we engaged in such a reflection by revisiting issues, by harnessing the most central research results for the benefit of practice, by illustrating principles and lessons (also from the history of algebra) to be taken into account in algebra education and by providing ideas for teachers' further reflection (which may result in enlightening exchanges among peers in teacher courses or teacher meetings). Many of the themes of this book may serve teachers and teacher educators for textbook analysis and selection, for choosing tasks and problems and for designing lesson plans (including the consideration of alternative pedagogical approaches to specific topics in algebra). Textbook writers and curriculum developers may also find useful materials and resources to inspire their work.

The core ideas highlighted in this book are summarized below and are suggested as central for ongoing reflection and discussion as well as the basis for future empirical studies and the morals to be derived from them.

Purposefulness

The practical orientation of most of today's students, coupled with the many competing stimuli (intellectual and others) to which they are exposed, make it imperative for teachers to be equipped with reasonable "answers" to the frequently asked question of "why algebra." This question can be addressed up front by making room for it in classrooms (of students and of future teachers alike) and by discussing plausible arguments of the kind developed in Chapter 1. Answers also can be based on purposefulness throughout algebra instruction by presenting meaningful and intellectually challenging problems which yield practically powerful and aesthetically pleasing results. We aimed at providing a sample of tasks (worked out or proposed) to be used as is or to serve as the inspiration for the development of new ones.

Essence

Alongside purposefulness and through repeated exposure to appropriate tasks, problems and discussions, students should gain a feel for what is the "essence" of algebra and its main entities (variables, expressions, equations and functions). Students and teachers should aim at subsuming the mastery of procedures to the essence of algebra and to develop that essence through meaningful, interesting and challenging non-routine ways (see examples throughout this book and especially in Chapter 4). Given the substantial reorientation that is required as students make the transition from arithmetic to algebra, there has been a great deal of interest in making early mathematical experiences a better preparation for algebra. In some instances, this means an earlier and hence more gradual introduction to working with algebraic letters and the algebraic entities described in Chapter 1. More commonly, however, the approach has been to bring the essence of algebra into earlier mathematics learning. The aim is to familiarize students with the core activities of algebra and the fundamental aspects of "algebraic thinking" well before formal work with algebraic notation begins. This approach fits with a broader movement to enrich mathematics by moving away from an emphasis on skills, to emphasize mathematical thinking and reasoning. Although this book has focused on algebra using symbols, the main tenets of this early algebra movement are also themes in the book, including developing a full understanding of equality as an equivalence relation, identifying patterns and expressing their generality, looking for mathematical structure and relationships, and recognizing functional dependence in situations.

Difficulties

Although adequate preparation may minimize difficulties, the transition from arithmetic to algebra entails considerable gaps and leaps imposed by the change of perspective and working tools. Chapter 3 describes in detail such difficulties, their possible origins and their inevitable nature and together with Chapter 4 it proposes strategies to cope with these difficulties. Chapter 5 also addresses the ways in which technology offers yet other tools to overcome those difficulties and suggests alternative learning trajectories. Teachers and teacher educators can try the proposals offered in these chapters first on themselves, then discuss them with peers and finally try them in classrooms, reporting back to peers and drawing conclusions and possibly further ideas of their own.

Tools

Mathematicians have always been using and developing tools. Chapter 2 illustrates the crucial role of notations and representations as intellectual tools that support advances in mathematics. Nowadays, digital tools for mathematics are becoming both sophisticated and accessible. This gives rise to the question of how digital technology may change, and in many countries continue to change, algebra education, including both its curricular content goals and its teaching and learning practices. Even if the learning gains of using digital tools for algebra seem to be limited to date, their potential for education is widely acknowledged. Exploiting this potential is a subtle pedagogical challenge. Even more challenging, however, is the curricular question: how much algebra knowledge is needed to be able to be a responsible citizen, a successful student in higher education and a competent professional in different fields? Answers to this question are the subject of an ongoing debate—however, it seems that higher order thinking skills (sometimes called the "21st century skills") will be decisive to prepare students for further careers as well as for life. As a consequence, a change of focus is occurring, reconsidering the role of procedural skills and highlighting strategic and analytic competences, using algebra for problem solving, and developing understanding. This process is ongoing worldwide, and the debate is expected to continue.

Heuristics Rather Than Prescriptions

Throughout the book, we aimed at unfolding ideas, complexities and possibilities. In spite of our human tendency to search for "how to" recommendations and precise prescriptive guidelines; we avoided them explicitly or implicitly. Rather, we suggested heuristics based on experiences accumulated through the years because they are more likely to be applicable to the many very different educational systems around the world. For example, we hinted at competing alternative entry points to algebra (e.g., expressions/functions first vs. equations first) and the intricate inter-relationships between algebraic procedures and algebraic objects.

Throughout the exposition as well as in the five "Thinking Further" sections, our goal was to have the readers experience for themselves the complexities and to develop a reflective and resourceful attitude towards them.

Coda

It is our hope that this book will be a small contribution to make the teaching of algebra, with all of its inherent complexities, viable, sustainable, and accessible to all and its learning productive and enjoyable.

INDEX

abstract elements 69–70
abstract problems 84–6
actions 4–11, 20–1
age of students 64
aims 1–4, 20–1
algebra: assistants 114, 117; definitions 2; derivation of word 1–2; value of 16–19, 21–2
Algebra Applet 115–16
Algebra Arrows 113, 119, 121
Algebra Balance Scales 122
algebraic expressions 13–14, 57; *see also* expressions
Algebra Trees 128
Analytic Art (Vieta) 37–8
Arabic mathematics 33–7, 45; geometric view of algebra 33–7, 45; al-Khwarizmi 33–7, 45, 76
Arcavi, A. 57–8, 72, 87–9, 93–4, 97–8
arithmetic 58–64, 75, 138
Arithmogon puzzles 74–5
authentic problems 81–6, 102–3
automatization 87

Babylonian mathematics 31–33
balance equation-solving model 67, 99, 121–2
Barbie Bungee activity 116–17, 119
blended learning 108

Boon, Peter 92
brackets, expansion 82, 99

calculation methods 4
CAS *see* computer algebra systems
"change side, change sign" mnemonic 75
changing numbers 119
CK *see* content knowledge
"closure" tendency 54
codes 50–1
completing the square 34, 40, 76
"complexifying" expressions 7
computer algebra systems (CAS) 112–15, 129, 132; differentiation error 71; equations 121–4; functions 125; symbolic functionality 110; variables 119–20, 132
content knowledge (CK) 80–1
context of teaching 81–6, 102–3
correction factor example 17–18
cover-up method 92–3, 128–9
creativity 64
critiquing arguments 18

decimal system 27
De Morgan, Augustus 39
denoting 5–6
dependency relationships 125
Descartes 60, 63

describing 5–6
developing concepts 115
difficulties: with technology 129, 133; transition from arithmetic 138
digital technology 106–35; appropriate tools/tasks 127–8; core entities 118–27, 132; teaching/learning algebra 127–30, 133–4; using fruitfully 127, 130
digital tools 108–17, 132, 138; functionality 109–13; good usage 127–30; pedagogical roles 114–17
diophantine equations 76
distributive property 96–7, 99
"do the same to both sides" strategy 66–7, 75–6, 121

Egyptian arithmetic 26–31, 42–5
elimination method, simultaneous equations 68
emphases in teaching 80–105
entities used in algebra 11–15, 20–1, 118–27, 132
equals sign 55–6, 74
equations 62–9; definitions 14–15; digital technology 120–4; equivalence 120, 123–4; expressions, confusion with 123; and functions 15; fundamental ideas 62–3; general strategy 62–3; graphical editors 109; linear 26–31; procedures 64–9, 75–7; rectangular 31–3; simultaneous 68–9; solving 62–9, 75–7, 99–101, 121–2; *see also* quadratic equations
equivalence 120, 123–4
essence of algebra 137–8
European mathematics 37–40, 46; algebraic rules 37–8; negative numbers 38–40, 46
Excel 111–12
exercise sequences 93–4
expanding brackets 82, 99
expressions: algebraic 13–14, 57; creating for purpose 10–11; equations, confusion with 123; mathematical structure 57; symbolic 6–8

False Position Rule 43–45
flexible thinking 72, 94

formulas 99–101, 125–6
Frend, William 38–40, 46
Freudenthal, H. 87, 92
Friedlander, A. 87–9, 93–4, 97
"fruit salad algebra" 51–3, 73, 95
functions: digital technology 111–16, 124–7, 132; and equations 15; examples of 124–5; as objects 116, 125; process-object duality 69–72, 77; tools, digital 111–13

games and puzzles 74–5, 86
generalizations: expressing 3; negative numbers 46; numbers 13, 119
GeoGebra software 111–13, 122, 124
geometric aspects: abstract problems 85–6; Arabic mathematics 33–7, 45; GeoGebra software 111–13, 122, 124
global substitution 129
graphical equation editors 109
graphing functionality 111
graphing technology 107, 111, 122–3, 132
graphs of functions 125–7
guess-check-improve methods 64–5, 108

heuristic learning/teaching 138–9
hieroglyphics 27
historical lessons 25–47
How to Solve it (Polya) 42

Information and Communication Technology (ICT) 109, 112, 116–17, 127, 133
input-output machines 124–5
insight 90–5, 103
instrumental genesis 129–30
Interactive White Boards (IWBs) 108

Japanese "shiki" 57

Keith, T. 43–4
al-Khwarizmi, Muhammad ibn Musa 33–7, 45, 76
Kindt, M. 87–90, 103
Koblitz, N. 19

learners 48–79; analysing work of others 97; conceptual structures 48;

differentiation error 71; difficulties with technology 129, 133; discussing mistakes 97–8; prior knowledge 50–1, 53–4; seeing through their eyes 48–79; student mistakes 95–9, 103
"letter-as-object" misconception 52, 95, 99
letters, representation 50–3, 73
linear equations 26–31
linearity illusion 96

massive open online courses (MOOCs) 106, 108
mathematical structure 56–8, 74–5
meaningful problems 81–6, 102–3
Mediant Inequality 4, 20
mistakes, student 95–9, 103
misuses of algebra 18–19
MOOCs *see* massive open online courses
De Morgan, Augustus 39
multiplication 27–9

naming the unknown 63
negative numbers 38–40, 46
nominalization 70
noticing 5–6
null factor law 76

objects: functions as 70–2, 116, 125; process-object duality 53–5, 67–72, 74, 77
online courses 106, 108
orchestrating learning 130

paper *see* pen-and-paper skills
Parallel Axes Representation (PAR) 9–10, 20–1
parameters 13, 119–20
pedagogical content knowledge (PCK) 80–1
pen-and-paper skills 107, 129, 130, 133
Perry, J. 45
placeholder variables 12, 118, 120
Polya, Georg 42
practice 87–90, 103, 115
prescriptive learning/teaching 138–9
Primary School Leaving Examinations (PSLE), Singapore 58–61, 75
The Principles of Algebra (Frend) 38

prior knowledge 50–1, 53–4
problem-solving 3, 58–61, 63
"procept" (process/object) concept 70, 72
process-object duality 53–5, 67–72, 74, 77
process view of functions 70, 72
productive practice 87–90, 103
proofs 4, 99–101, 103–4
properties 3–4, 28–9
proving theorems 4
PSLE *see* Primary School Leaving Examinations
purposefulness 137
puzzles and games 74–5, 86

quadratic equations: Babylonian mathematics 31–3; difficulties with technology 129; solving 76, 99–101
quadratic expressions 57

Ray, Joseph 51–2
"reading" expressions 7–8
real life problems 81–6, 102–3
rectangular equations 31–3
rectangular expanding brackets model 82, 99
reification 69–70
relations 3, 15, 55–6
representation 5–6; connections 8–10; digital technology 112–13, 125–8; functions 125–6; historical lessons 27–8, 31, 41; letters 50–3, 73; PAR 9–10, 20–1
Rhind Papyrus 26, 29–31, 42–3, 65
"roots", al-Khwarizmi 33–7, 45, 125
routine 90–5, 103
Rule of the False Position 43–5
rules, algebraic 37–8

sequential line entry 110
Sfard, A. 69, 71
Sherpa orchestration 130, 133
"shiki" (mathematical expressions) 57
signs 11–12
simultaneous equations 68–9
Singapore 58–61, 75
skills: pen-and-paper 107, 129, 130, 133; practising 115
"squares", al-Khwarizmi 33–7, 45

structure of mathematics 56–8, 74–5
student mistakes 95–9, 103; *see also* learners
symbolic expressions 6–8
symbolic functionality 109–10
symbolic representations 126–127

table functionality 112
tables of values 125–6
teachers 48, 49
technology *see* digital technology
theorems, proving 4
Think Of A Number (THOAN) problems 85
tools 138; *see also* digital tools

"unclosed" expressions 56
undoing operations 65–7, 75–6, 120–1
unknown numbers 12, 63, 77, 119, 120
unsymbolizing 7–8

variables: digital technology 118–20, 132; facets 12–13, 70, 118–20
varying quantities 70, 112–13, 119
Vieta, Franciscus 37–8, 42, 60
visualization 112–13

Whig history 41
white boards 108
Whitehead, Alfred North 46

# Taylor & Francis eBooks

Helping you to choose the right eBooks for your Library

Add Routledge titles to your library's digital collection today. Taylor and Francis ebooks contains over 50,000 titles in the Humanities, Social Sciences, Behavioural Sciences, Built Environment and Law.

Choose from a range of subject packages or create your own!

Benefits for you
- Free MARC records
- COUNTER-compliant usage statistics
- Flexible purchase and pricing options
- All titles DRM-free.

Benefits for your user
- Off-site, anytime access via Athens or referring URL
- Print or copy pages or chapters
- Full content search
- Bookmark, highlight and annotate text
- Access to thousands of pages of quality research at the click of a button.

 Free Trials Available
We offer free trials to qualifying academic, corporate and government customers.

eCollections – Choose from over 30 subject eCollections, including:

Archaeology	Language Learning
Architecture	Law
Asian Studies	Literature
Business & Management	Media & Communication
Classical Studies	Middle East Studies
Construction	Music
Creative & Media Arts	Philosophy
Criminology & Criminal Justice	Planning
Economics	Politics
Education	Psychology & Mental Health
Energy	Religion
Engineering	Security
English Language & Linguistics	Social Work
Environment & Sustainability	Sociology
Geography	Sport
Health Studies	Theatre & Performance
History	Tourism, Hospitality & Events

For more information, pricing enquiries or to order a free trial, please contact your local sales team:
www.tandfebooks.com/page/sales

 The home of Routledge books

www.tandfebooks.com